AF322701

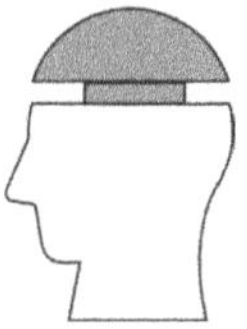

Praise for *RESET Leader*

"On my first day as Managing Director for Southwest Europe, we launched the leadership Growth Mindset Accelerator. We were entering a major business transformation, and I wanted leaders to start with the right mindset and a shared way of working across Spain, France, and Italy. What followed was not a program, but a fundamental transformation of how we relate to each other, drive change and learn as an organization. RESET became an ongoing rhythm, supported by internal mentors who had gone through earlier Accelerators and now help teams shift mindsets and turn insight into action. It empowers change at speed and builds leadership capability where it matters most."

—Martina Müller
Managing Director at FrieslandCampina (South West Europe)

"The work is highly practical and impactful, and it challenges you to confront the key barriers that hold progress back—often starting

with yourself. Using a RESET rhythm supported by a data-driven mindset diagnosis, we created a quarterly cycle of reflection, prioritization, tracking, and forward movement. This proved highly effective in strengthening alignment within our leadership team and delivering ambitious goals, even amid very challenging external conditions."

—Joost Houben
Commercial Lead Foods Benelux &
Head of Sales The Netherlands at Unilever

"Mindset isn't optional—it's critical. We knew old behaviours wouldn't deliver the results we were aiming for. This work pushed me well outside my comfort zone and created a level of vulnerability and psychological safety where real issues could be confronted in the moment. That depth is what makes the difference. This isn't a tick-box program or a new management idea—it's fundamental psychology."

—Will Jones
Managing Director at FrieslandCampina (United Kingdom & Ireland)

"One thing I've learned leading across the Americas is that you can't use a one-size-fits-all approach. The mindset assessments really opened my eyes—they pushed me to stop leading based on my own assumptions and start leading based on where my team actually is. It gave us a clear picture of our individual strengths and a roadmap for how to grow together. Integrating the RESET Leader *method has turned into our go-to way to recalibrate and keep everyone moving in the right direction. It's been huge for building clarity and getting things done faster."*

—Sumeet Mathur
Managing Director at FrieslandCampina (Americas)

"One of the things we're doing is embedding Growth Mindset principles within the team. We think of it as a platform that encourages talent to share learnings—not just the wins, but also the challenges and different ways of doing things. That helps accelerate learning and allows insights to cascade quickly across our innovation. Partnering with Growthstars has been helpful in strengthening the muscle around taking calculated risks, embracing learning through failure, and creating the culture needed for future success."

—Amir Kazmi
Former Chief Information & Digital Officer at Westrock
Current Chief Tech & Growth Officer at Ralliant

"Our growth ambition was significant—and the targets were demanding. We had a strong, capable leadership team, but speed mattered. We needed to move fast, together. What we were missing was a shared language and clear ways of working that could support that pace. Growthstars gave us exactly that: practical tools, meaningful experiences, and a structured way to begin building the culture we needed to achieve our goals."

—Daryn Edgar
Former CEO of LYTT, a BP Company
Current CEO of Edmonton Global

"My initial skepticism was that Growth Mindset might be another management concept that comes and goes. Instead, it proved to be refreshingly practical. It challenged how we think as leaders and as teams, while allowing us to experiment in small, safe steps before taking bigger leaps. It helped people reconnect with

feeling, learning fast, and acting boldly. That combination made the change real."

—Kevin de Wolf
Former President & CFO at FrieslandCampina (Americas)
Current Managing Director Doka (USA)

"What stood out was the thoughtful mix of full-team working sessions, individual coaching, and sub-team journey segments. Most importantly, the experiments between sessions mattered. You consistently challenged me to try new behaviors—some uncomfortable at first—which have since become part of my daily leadership practice. That combination of real usefulness and genuine enjoyment is what made the journey stick."

—Stefan Pfeifer
Managing Director Germany at Unilever

"Growthstars created a structured opportunity for self-reflection—on how we perform, the mindsets we bring into conversations, and whether we're truly maximizing opportunities. From idea to scale-up is a long journey with different challenges, and you need different tools along the way. What stood out was the systematic approach: clear objectives at both individual and collective levels, frequent check-ins, and visible progress week by week. It created stronger collaboration and a common language around growth."

—Tommy Langnes
Former Co-Founder & Chief Business
Development Officer at LYTT, a BP Company
Currently the CEO & Co-founder of Lightsonic

"This work forced me to unlearn deeply ingrained leadership habits—leading top-down and stepping in to do things myself when we hit resistance. Through the process, I became aware of Fixed Mindsets I didn't realise I was still carrying. Shifting from 'know-it-all' to 'learn-it-all' changed how I lead and created real agility in the business. More importantly, it connected me back to the kind of legacy I want to leave—not just amplifying myself, but helping others grow and succeed."

—Wayne Thompson
Former Business Unit Controller
at FrieslandCampina (United Kingdom & Ireland)
Currently Head of Lakeland Dairies (United Kingdom)

"Mindsets are difficult to spot and easy to misunderstand. What made the difference here was turning mindset into action—clear behaviors, practical habits, and simple exercises that people could apply every day. That's how progress stopped being abstract and started delivering real results."

—Jesus de Antonio
HR Director for Spain, Italy, and France,
FrieslandCampina (South West Europe)

"As a leadership coach working with the 6 Types of Working Genius and other personality tools has been powerful in helping leaders and their teams. What I saw missing was a way to translate that insight into sustained behavioral change under pressure. Using 8Star Mindset Assessment with my clients has filled this gap. It fosters deep self-awareness of a Growth Mindset and the barriers that limit it, and turns insight into focused action. What I appreciate about

RESET Leader *is how quickly it gives clients concrete tools to use week by week in real-time situations. That's where I've seen transformation happen and the impact stick."*

—Josh Simmons
Principal, Spark Genius Consulting

What I've seen through working with RESET Leader *is how that insight finally translates into development.* RESET Leader *doesn't try to change people's personality; it helps leaders work deliberately on understanding learned mindsets and behaviors—unlearning what no longer serves them and reinforcing what does. Using the 8Star Mindset Assessments, I've seen this shift show up in real work, across teams and contexts, which is why* RESET Leader *has become a meaningful part of how I support leaders and organizations."*

—Edwin van Vianen
Principal, Next By Design

RESET Leader

RESET Leader

Shift Mindsets.
Activate Strategy.
Deliver Results.

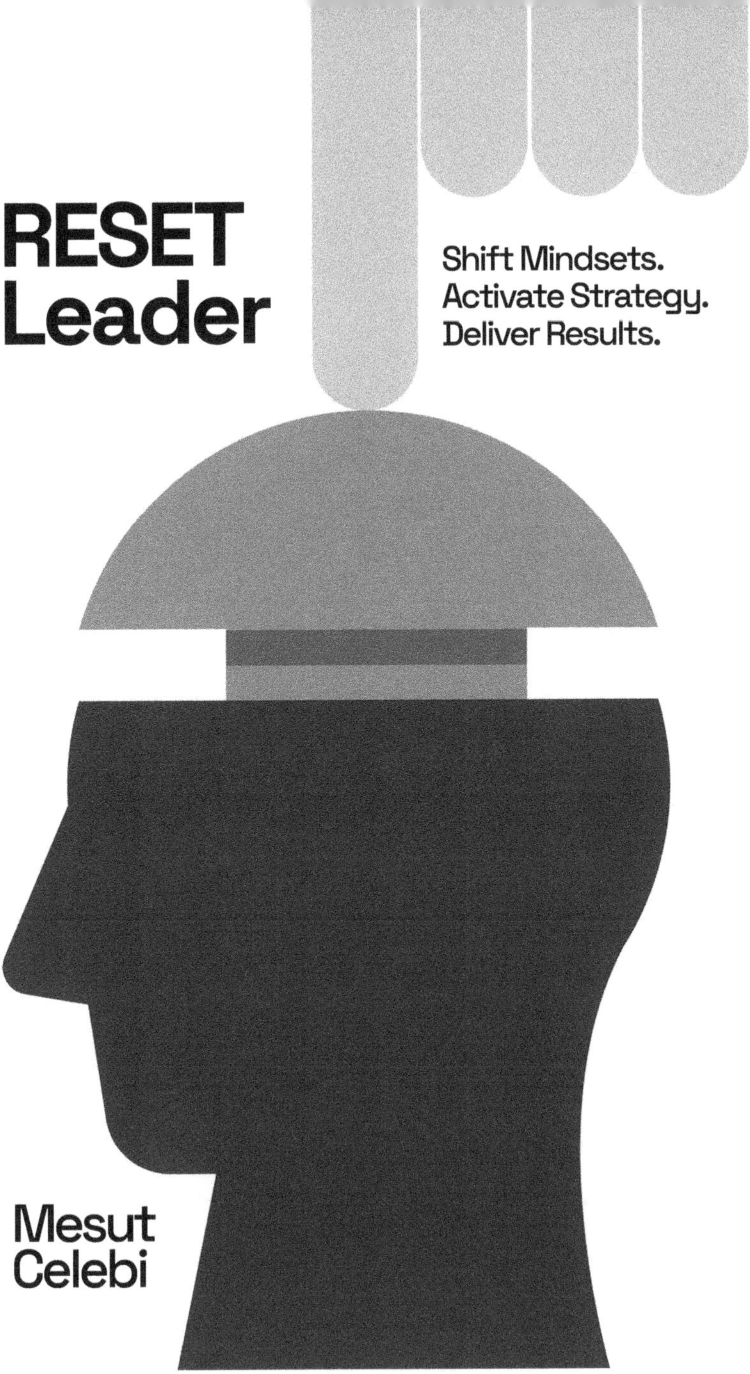

Mesut
Celebi

Publish Your Purpose
141 Weston Street, #155
Hartford, CT, 06141

Ordering Information: Quantity sales and special discounts are available on quantity purchases by corporations, associations, and others. For details, contact the author at hello@growthstars.co.

Edited by: Elliot Tapia-Kwan, August Li, Alexander Loutsenko, Lily Capstick
Cover design by: Gil Shuler
Typeset by: Medlar Publishing Solutions Pvt Ltd

ISBN: 979-8-88797-229-9 (hardcover)
ISBN: 979-8-88797-230-5 (paperback)
ISBN: 979-8-88797-231-2 (ebook)

Library of Congress Control Number: 2026902220

First edition, May 2026.

Publish Your Purpose is a hybrid publisher of nonfiction books. Our mission is to elevate the voices often excluded from traditional publishing. We intentionally seek out authors and storytellers with diverse backgrounds, life experiences, and unique perspectives to publish books that will make an impact in the world. Do you have a book idea you would like us to consider publishing? Please visit PublishYourPurpose.com for more information.

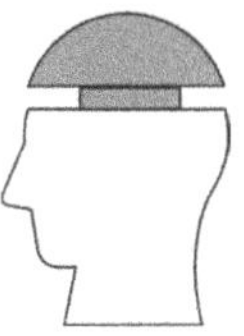

Dedication

To Patrick de Zeeuw, friend and partner, whose spark ignited this journey. Your belief, imagination, and friendship helped shape the early path that made *RESET Leader* possible. Your impact continues far beyond your time with us.

To my children, Ella Noor, Arman, and Imre, from whom I have learned far more than they have from me. Their authenticity, curiosity, and resilience have been my greatest teachers.

And to Rieke, who has walked beside me through most of my life and entrepreneurial journey. Thank you for listening to the endless ideas, ventures, and experiments as they took shape, and for being a steady advisor in the background through every evolution.

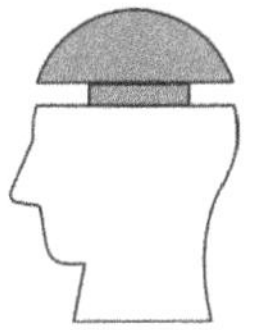

Contents

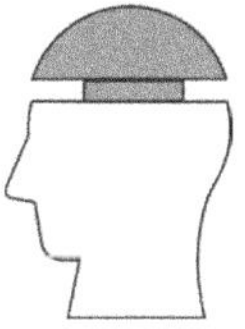

Foreword

I met Mesut in 2019, during a time when we were facing a challenge many large organizations will recognize. Despite our scale, experience, and resources, we were being outpaced by smaller, faster competitors. Our ideas were strong, but our ability to translate them into results was not. What once took us one and a half to two years to bring new ideas to market no longer matched the pace around us, and frustration was growing.

In response, we created dedicated teams and experimented with more entrepreneurial ways of working. Some initiatives showed promise—yet time and again, progress stalled when they re-entered the core organization. The challenge was not a lack of effort or intent. Instead, something essential was missing when new approaches collided with entrenched ways of thinking.

During this period, our senior leadership team encountered fresh perspectives on learning and leadership. Through conversations with Mesut, we realized that our true constraint wasn't knowledge or capability, but ingrained thinking patterns—especially under pressure. RESET gave us the language and structure to address this, focusing not on adding tools, but on helping leaders fundamentally rethink their approach to change.

RESET Leader made tangible the connection between personal growth and organizational execution. When leaders shift how they think, organizations shift how they perform. This work is about breaking limiting patterns and replacing them with habits that support progress where it matters most.

Having led many change efforts over the years, I can say this work truly stood out. RESET helped us accelerate adaptation—not just at the top, but deep within teams where change often stalls. It provided a clear way to make change personal, uncover hidden barriers, and shift underlying mindsets into sustained behavior. What made it especially powerful was how quickly it translated into real business outcomes: faster execution, sharper decision-making, and greater ownership across the organization.

One key insight that stayed with me was our shift from treating mindset change as a top-down push to enabling a bottom-up pull. Much like VO_2 Max in endurance training, where athletes track their capacity to perform, RESET helped our leaders recognize and build their own growth readiness. This made mindset visible and, more importantly, something people genuinely wanted to improve. That energy shift—from compliance to ownership—proved to be a real turning point.

The journey is not easy. It requires leaders to challenge old habits, embrace continuous learning, and resist the comfort of familiar certainties. *RESET Leader* captures what this looks like in practice—and why it is essential for organizations seeking to remain relevant and resilient.

This book reflects lessons learned the hard way—inside a complex organization under real pressure. I believe it will resonate with leaders who understand that, today, change demands more than intelligence or speed. It demands the ability to reset how we lead.

Tuncay Özgüner
President, Retail & Americas
FrieslandCampina

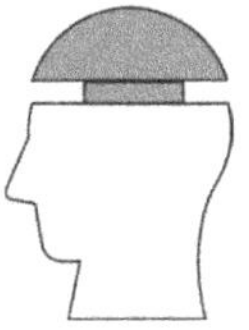

Introduction

The Mountaintop Gives Us Perspective. The Valley is Where Things Actually Change

I didn't understand this at first despite the fact I experienced it—over and over—in business, and life. The mountaintop is where vision is born; the valley is where vision gets tested under pressure. That's where habits surface, pressure shows up, and leadership becomes personal. Today, change moves faster than ever, leaders are constantly moving between these two places. Learning to navigate that movement—without losing yourself or your people—is where leadership really begins.

The *RESET Leader* philosophy grew out of this rhythm—the continual ascent toward clarity and the descent into growth. In every transformation I've witnessed, whether in a multinational boardroom or a start-up sprint, the real breakthroughs didn't come from new strategies alone but from leaders who had the courage to confront themselves in the valley. Not in a dramatic way, but in very practical moments: When pressure rises, habits take over, and old ways no longer work. It's there that habits actually shift. And when enough of them do, culture follows.

Leadership today demands the capacity to pause before climbing again. Not to strategize—to actually reflect on what just happened. What I've seen is that this pause is often the hardest part—especially when pressure is high and everything in you wants to move faster. This book is an invitation to embrace that cycle—not as a crisis to survive but as a discipline to master. A way of working with change, instead of constantly reacting to it. Whether you're guiding a global enterprise or leading yourself through change, the lessons ahead are designed to help you navigate both the mountain and the valley in a way that is actually sustainable when things get hard.

If this book found its way to you, chances are that you already sense that something isn't working the way it used to. The strategy may be sound, the ambition real, and yet the execution feels heavier, alignments more fragile, and change harder to sustain than it should be.

Many of us experience this quietly—not because we lack capability or conviction, but because the world around us has accelerated faster than the habits, beliefs, and systems we've relied on for years. When pressure rises, those habits take over before we even notice it happening. That tension—between knowing what needs to change and feeling how difficult it is to make it stick—is not a personal failure. It's the starting point. Every meaningful transformation I've witnessed begins exactly there.

The Journey that Brought Me Here

I didn't set out to build a company like Growthstars. In many ways, it was the natural result of a journey that's taken me across industries, continents, and countless moments of learning and unlearning. At the time, it didn't feel like a journey at all—just a series of choices that made sense in the moment. I started out in the Netherlands, in the packaging industry: a world of precision, production lines, and tangible results. But even then, what fascinated me most wasn't the process of making things. It was understanding what makes *people* come alive: what drives them to grow and create something meaningful together.

That curiosity led me to entrepreneurship. In 1999, I founded my first company, and over the next two decades, I helped build and scale ventures in industrial technology, manufacturing, and software across Europe, Africa, and the Middle East. Every chapter brought new lessons—not only about business, but about human behavior. I saw brilliant strategies fail because teams weren't aligned, and average ideas succeed because people believed in them deeply. Seeing that gap—between logic and what actually happened—was frustrating. Growth, I began to understand, has less to do with structure and more to do with mindset.

There was a period when I believed that if the strategy was clear enough and the logic strong enough, people would follow. On paper, it all made sense. I had seen too many smart plans stall, too many transformations lose momentum, and too many capable leaders grow frustrated—myself included!

I wasn't missing intelligence, experience, or ambition, so I asked: What *is* missing?

The answer to this question came into focus over time: An honest understanding of how deeply unspoken fears shape behavior under pressure—fears tied to identity, to habits we don't even see as habits anymore. I didn't yet have language for it, but I could feel the disconnect: between what we *knew* needed to change and what we were actually *able* to change. That realization didn't come from a breakthrough workshop or a new framework. It came from sitting in the discomfort of the valley: watching execution lag and resistance surface, I started realizing that leadership required a different kind of reset than I had been applying.

When I moved to New York in 2009, that insight deepened. I didn't just change countries; I stepped into a different level of speed and ambition. I co-founded Startupbootcamp USA, a global accelerator helping entrepreneurs turn bold ideas into reality. Later, as a senior partner at Innoleaps, I worked with some of the world's largest enterprises, from Heineken, Unilever to Georgia-Pacific, guiding their innovation efforts. Whether in a start-up or a multinational, the same truth kept surfacing: Strategies don't fail for lack of intelligence; they fail because behaviors don't change fast enough—especially when the pace increases and old habits feel safer than new ones

That realization became the foundation for what I now call the **RESET framework**: a simple, structured way for leaders to see what's actually holding them back—and to do something about it, in small steps, before the old patterns take over again. This framework took shape because we needed a practical way to work with what I was seeing again and again. It's not theory; it's the distillation of years spent watching people, teams, and organizations try—and often struggle—to change.

As *RESET Leader* matured into an operating system, it became clear that it could not live only in workshops or moments of intervention. What we kept seeing at Growthstars was that momentum faded once people returned to their day-to-day reality. For change to *stick*, leaders needed continuity: continuity across roles, across teams, and across organizational layers, and they needed this over time. The system had to follow people as they grew and reset *repeatedly*. That requirement shaped how RESET evolved in practice, ensuring that reflection and guidance remained available not just at the start of a transformation, but throughout the learning journey.

Today, through Growthstars and *RESET Leader*, our focus is on helping leaders and teams close the gap between vision and behavior, and bring strategy to life in the way they think and act every day. Not in the abstract, but in the moments when pressure is real and habits tend to take over. Because leadership isn't just about climbing higher; it's about learning to transform in the valleys along the way.

The Speed of Change and the Need for Adaptability

Change is constant. While we've always known this, the pace at which change unfolds today is unprecedented. What feels different now is how quickly that change shows up in our day-to-day reality. Historically, change spanned generations, allowing societies to adjust gradually. Stability was a virtue, and tradition, hierarchy, and long-term planning defined how industries and communities operated. But technological advancements and globalization have compressed these cycles. Change that once took decades now happens within months, reshaping industries and careers. Navigating this acceleration is no longer optional; it's a critical skill ... especially when speed leaves little room for reflection.

I've experienced this firsthand. Growing up as the child of Kurdish immigrants in the Netherlands, I constantly navigated the clash between my family's traditions and the external world's expectations. Later, after moving to New York City with my own family, I faced a similar but intensified challenge—this time with higher stakes. It wasn't just a professional shift; it questioned how I saw myself and where I belonged. Professionally, I reinvented myself without the cushion of a stable job, stepping into the unknown. Everything changed: what we ate, how we communicated, our social norms, and our sense of belonging. It was a complete reset.

Change rarely stays external—it quickly becomes personal, challenging our beliefs and values. Resistance, both internal and external, naturally arises. Friends, colleagues, and even loved ones may push back against our growth, consciously or unconsciously. We see the same dynamic play out inside organizations: Resistance is the leading reason why transformations, whether M&As or operational overhauls fail. Yet, I've learned that resistance isn't an obstacle; it's information. It shows you exactly where habits and identity are being tested. Growth demands that we balance effort with surrender, taking action while staying with discomfort long enough for something new to emerge.

The world is moving faster than my ability to absorb it. Astro Teller, Director of Google X, captures this reality: "The rate of technological change is now accelerating so fast that it has risen above the average rate at which most people can absorb it." Not just with rapidly evolving technology, but also the ways in which we interact, how our culture evolves, and the day-to-day cycles of how we do business. I also feel overwhelmed at times—and yet I realize that the world won't slow down for me.

Thomas Friedman, a Pulitzer Prize-winning journalist and global affairs commentator adds, "When the pace of change gets this fast, the only way to retain a lifelong working capacity is to engage in lifelong learning." What started as a theoretical concept for me eventually grew into a deep personal commitment—not just to keep up with the rat race, but to look ahead to a *desirable* future. What we see across organizations is that many fall behind, not because they lack intelligence or ambition, but because they cling to outdated routines: "This is how we do things here."

These ingrained patterns create a false sense of stability. Change rarely announces itself; it isn't always loud or obvious. Sometimes it creeps in subtly until, *suddenly,* entire industries are transformed. The COVID-19 pandemic, originating from a single city, disrupted global norms at unprecedented speed, and fundamentally changed how business was done—at least for a few years. Then after OpenAI's ChatGPT revolutionized AI, it was challenged within a very short time by new players like DeepSeek and many others.

The challenge isn't predicting change, it's preparing for it. And it starts within: by noticing what you do when things speed up, questioning the status quo, embracing discomfort, and choosing to keep learning even when old habits feel safer.

CHAPTER ONE

On Growth Mindset and the Journey of Learning

While my children were growing and attending school, I came across Carol Dweck's work on Growth Mindset in an unexpected way, through conversations with my children about their schoolwork. I noticed how much emphasis was placed on grades rather than learning, so I began experimenting with shifting the conversation from results to the journey. Instead of asking, *"What grade did you get?"* I started asking, *"What did you learn?"* It was eye-opening. Focusing on the process helped my children approach challenges with curiosity and resilience rather than fear of failure. Over time, something I had sensed intuitively came into sharper focus—learning isn't about comfort, it's about *stretching* just beyond it. Growth happens when safety and gratitude give us the courage to stretch into the unknown. This simple shift mirrored what I was observing in leadership and entrepreneurship; success wasn't about having the perfect answer but about staying committed to the process of learning.

That's when it became clear to me: Growth Mindset isn't just an enabler for learning, it's the foundation for handling any form of change. As I explored how it could be applied to business, this concept became central to my work, especially when addressing innovation and growth. I saw that *learning agility,* the willingness to learn, unlearn, and relearn, is one of the most critical building blocks of transformation. Startups demonstrate this beautifully. They don't evolve just because markets shift—they evolve because they believe in something new and are willing to iterate until they get there.

I saw this firsthand while working with startups at Startupbootcamp, now one of the world's top startup accelerators, where I was a founding partner for the Americas branch. Startups operate in an environment of rapid change, where they must iterate and evolve in real time. To survive, they rely on accelerators, mentors, and structured processes designed to maximize learning speed. The same principles apply to leadership: Success isn't about following a linear path but about continuously adjusting and learning in an accelerated way. Throughout our ten hubs around the globe, we received thousands of applications from startups eager to join our accelerators. We weren't just looking for innovative ideas, we were looking for people deeply passionate about their vision, yet open-minded enough to learn, adapt, and pivot when necessary. Striking this balance between conviction and flexibility is equally essential for organizations aiming to drive meaningful transformation.

It was during a visit to San Francisco, while attending the Lean Startup Conference, that my then-partner Patrick de Zeeuw and I began a conversation that would later become the foundation of *RESET Leader*. We asked ourselves: *What is the one mindset and behavior that encompasses all others? How can we bring this not only to our own group of companies but also to the hundreds of startups we accelerated?* This conversation planted the seeds for what would eventually evolve into a structured approach to helping individuals and organizations embrace transformation and embed learning agility into the fabric of leadership and business growth.

What are Mindsets?

Mindsets are the internal operating systems that shape how we perceive ourselves, others, and the world. They are not just beliefs we *hold*—they are the beliefs that *hold us*, quietly guiding how we interpret events and make decisions. Like lenses in a pair of glasses, mindsets filter reality. Depending on the lens, the same situation can look like a threat or an opportunity, a setback or a signal to grow. Because these mental frameworks run largely in the background, we often act on them long before we recognize they're at play.

Psychologists describe mindsets as cognitive frameworks formed by the experiences we accumulate, the environments we move through, and the narratives we come to believe about ourselves and others. These inputs create mental shortcuts that help us interpret complexity and make quick judgments in daily life. Over time, these shortcuts become the default patterns through which we process challenges and opportunities. In themselves, these patterns are adaptive; they help us navigate a complex world efficiently. When left unexamined under conditions of threat or fear, they can solidify into habits that limit learning, and collaboration. But when brought into awareness, mindsets become a powerful lever for change—something we can question, reshape, and use to drive meaningful transformation.

While our personality—what many might refer to as our "nature"—forms the stable core of how we are wired, mindsets belong to the realm of "nurture." Personality assessments such as MBTI, DiSC, CliftonStrengths, the Big Five, Facet5, the Enneagram, and newer tools like Working Genius reveal our natural tendencies. They show us how we prefer to think, interact, decide, and find energy in our work. These traits are often remarkably stable over time and tend to feel innate, like they are God-given in their consistency. But personality alone does not determine how we lead or adapt. That part lives in *nurture*—the beliefs, interpretations, and assumptions we accumulate through our experiences. Mindsets sit here. They are *learned lenses* shaped by environment, challenge, culture, and meaning-making. Unlike personality, which remains relatively constant, mindsets can be intentionally examined and reshaped.

Tools like the **8Star** mindset assessment were designed specifically to reveal these learned patterns—highlighting growth barriers and identifying where shifts can unlock new behavior. At Growthstars, we developed the 8Star mindset assessment to make recurring mindset patterns visible and actionable, giving leaders and teams a shared language to recognize barriers and support real behavior change.

A helpful way to think about mindsets is to imagine them as the "default settings" of a device. Most people try to change their behaviors—prioritizing differently, communicating more clearly—without realizing the default settings are still running in the background. This creates friction, inconsistency, and frustration. But when leaders intentionally update their mindset, the behavioral change that once felt forced or fragile becomes natural and sustainable. Mindset doesn't just influence what we do; it sets the conditions for what we believe is possible.

Understanding what mindsets are is the first step; the next is noticing how they shape our behavior in real time, especially in moments that matter.

Mindsets in Action: Behavior as an Outcome of Perspective

The power of mindsets lies in how they shape the choices we make and the actions we take. They influence everything from how we approach challenges to how we perceive the success of others. These mental lenses, whether empowering or limiting, determine how we interpret and respond to the situations we encounter daily.

To better understand how these mental lenses function in practice, we turn to the extensive research of Dr. Carol Dweck, a leading psychologist whose work has transformed how we think about human potential. Her groundbreaking studies reveal that mindsets are pivotal in shaping not only individual growth but also organizational success. Dweck identifies two primary types of mindsets that drive behavior: Fixed Mindsets and Growth Mindsets.

Mindsets act as the foundation for our responses to critical moments. For instance, how do we react when faced with a significant challenge? Do we avoid it for fear of failure, or do we see it as an opportunity to learn? Similarly, how do we perceive the success of others? Do we feel inspired or threatened? These patterns of thought stem from our mindsets, often without us even realizing it. Recognizing these patterns is the first step toward understanding how our mindsets influence not just our own actions, but the culture of our teams and organizations.

Over time, through our work with leaders and teams, I came to understand that true adaptability isn't about reacting to change; it's about choosing a mindset that allows you to continuously reset and grow.

Breakthrough Realizations and the Birth of RESET

Throughout my life, I've encountered groundbreaking insights that fundamentally shaped how I approach leadership, growth, and transformation. Two stand out in particular, one from my career as an entrepreneur and another from my deep dive into human behavior.

Entrepreneurship Is Not About Nature— It Can Be Learned

There's a common belief that entrepreneurs are born, not made, that successful founders have an inherent, almost genetic, ability to spot opportunities, and build businesses. But my experience at Startupbootcamp and Innoleaps proved otherwise. Time and time again, I saw aspiring founders, some with no prior entrepreneurial background, grow into resilient, adaptable leaders. What made the difference wasn't talent alone, but their willingness to learn, to let go of what no longer worked, and evolve at an incredible pace.

This realization shattered the myth that entrepreneurship is purely a matter of nature. **It's not about who we are when we start (our nature), it's about how we grow along the way (our nurture).** And this is true far beyond startups; it applies to leadership at every level.

Behavior Can Be Changed by Identifying Mindsets

If being entrepreneurial can be learned, what about leadership? What about the ability to embrace change rather than resist it? This led me to my second major realization: **Behavioral change isn't just about skill-building, it's about shifting mindset.**

Throughout our work coaching executives, and scaling businesses, we began to notice the same patterns repeating:

- When people struggled with change, it wasn't due to lack of resources, strategy, or intelligence. It was because their underlying mindsets held them back.
- When leaders failed to adapt, it wasn't a lack of capability. It was a rigid belief system preventing them from seeing new possibilities.
- And when organizations hit growth barriers, the root cause was rarely a process problem; it was a people problem, shaped by the mindsets driving behavior.

This was a turning point. If mindset is at the core of behavior, then the key to transformation isn't just **teaching new skills**, it's **resetting mindsets** to unlock new ways of thinking and acting.

Over time, I saw a deeper pattern emerge: Every breakthrough began with discomfort. The people who grew the most were not those who avoided the valley, but those who learned to move through it intentionally—to pause, reflect, and reset.

The Foundations of Becoming a RESET Leader

At the heart of becoming a RESET leader is the ability to keep learning while everything around you is moving. That sounds simple. It isn't. Traditional leadership approaches relied on stability and predictability, but today's workplace demands leaders who can continuously reset their thinking, habits, and behaviors to meet evolving challenges. I can't stress this enough: Not everyone needs to be an entrepreneur, but in times of rapid change, everyone needs to *think entrepreneurially.* The ability to keep learning—especially when the ground is shifting—is no longer a nice-to-have.

This is where the RESET framework comes in. Through working with hundreds of teams, across startups, scale-ups, and enterprises in a wide range of industries, we began to see a consistent thread: Sustainable growth and transformation require more than just strategy. They demand a structured approach to overcoming internal barriers and shifting mindsets. The RESET framework provides this structure—not as a one-time solution, but as a continuous rhythm of learning and execution. It helps leaders recognize when they are on the mountain and when they are in the valley, and to move between the two with intention. The framework consists of five key steps:

- **R - Recognize Growth Barriers:** Spot the patterns and behaviors that no longer serve you, the habits that slow momentum and hold you back from executing your strategy.
- **E - Evaluate Mindset Shifts:** Look beneath the surface. Identify the forces that shape those behaviors and reframe them to open new pathways for growth.
- **S - Set Up Habit-Shifting Experiments:** Turn intention into action. Design small, bold tests and practices to challenge old routines and build new ways of working.
- **E - Examine New Behavior Impact:** Pause to learn. Measure what's changing, notice what's working, and refine what moves you closer to meaningful progress.

- **T – Transform Successful Habits into New Working Rituals:** Make changes stick. Embed the habits that drive success into your rhythm, culture, and daily leadership practices.

Each step is designed to build on the previous one, creating a cycle of continous experimantation and learning. These aren't abstract concepts; they're actionable, and designed to be applied in real-world leadership situations.

Why are these steps so impactful for RESET Leaders? Because transformation isn't just about external change; it's about reshaping how we *think* and *respond* when we're under pressure. Growth barriers often stem from deeply ingrained mindsets, beliefs like *This is how we've always done it* or *That will never work here*. RESET helps leaders recognize these limiting patterns, shift their thinking, and experiment with new approaches, enabling them to lead with greater agility and adaptability.

Over the years, as an entrepreneur and executive coach, I've worked with leaders across startups, multinational corporations, and nonprofits. No matter the context, the same pattern kept surfacing: the biggest obstacle to growth isn't the change itself—it's our ability to reset our mindset in response to it. Leaders who embrace the RESET framework stop reacting and start experimenting. That shift—from defense to curiosity—changes everything downstream.

That's why this book focuses on applying RESET to leadership and transformation. The workplace is where deeply ingrained mindsets shape decision-making, and ultimately, organizational success. By shifting from a reactive to a proactive mindset, leaders can break through inertia, foster environments where teams can thrive.

RESET Leaders aren't just navigating change; they're driving it, shaping the future with adaptability and vision. They're leaders who make it safe to learn—and who keep learning themselves, especially when the pressure says to stop. These leadership qualities are rooted in one core truth: Mindset shifts fuel lasting transformation. Throughout this book, we'll not only explore the five steps of the RESET framework but also learn how to embody the mindset shifts that make transformation possible.

But none of this happens unless we understand what's actually shaping how we think—especially the parts we'd rather not look at. The RESET framework provides the roadmap for change, but the journey begins within. Without addressing the internal barriers that hold us back, even the best strategies can falter. That's where the eight core growth areas come in, illuminating the mindsets that either hinder or accelerate growth.

These growth areas show the challenges individuals face in adapting to change and how shifting ingrained mindsets unlock new possibilities. They are woven into each chapter, providing a deeper lens into how mindset transformation happens in real-world leadership and organizational contexts.

The world needs more **RESET Leaders**—those who can lead with adaptability and inspire others to do the same. Whether in business, communities, or personal life, these individuals keep seeing what needs to shift—in themselves first, and then around them. Not once. Over and over. Because change doesn't stop.

And this is not just a call to action—it is an invitation, perhaps even a calling. Growth isn't achieved through effort alone. It requires something harder: the willingness to let go of what you can't control. Faith—whether in God or a higher power—often plays a vital role in helping people navigate uncertainty and welcome growth. We are not meant to walk this journey alone. True RESET Leaders understand that transformation demands more than action—it calls for trust—the kind that shows up when you step into something without knowing how it ends.

As you read this book, I invite you to not only **become a RESET Leader** but also to **seek out those who embody this spirit**. These leaders exist in many spaces. They are shaping the future, often without recognition. If you pay close attention, you will see, hear, *and* recognize their impact.

I've come to see that we don't grow only through plans and strategies; we grow through cycles—of seeing clearly, being stretched, and resetting again. The valleys of change can be humbling, but they are also where we discover what truly endures. Whether you lead a team, a business, or a family, transformation begins when you stop resisting the valley and start walking through it.

The mountaintop inspires us. The valley transforms us.

CHAPTER TWO

Recognizing Growth Barriers

Every leadership team meticulously formulates its three-year plan, ensuring that their mission aligns with broader organizational goals. This careful process of aligning aspirations creates a shared vision and sets the foundation for future success. However, despite the clarity and dedication poured into these strategic plans, we often overlook a crucial aspect—what might get in the way once execution begins. What often goes unnoticed are the subtle yet significant challenges that arise within day-to-day operations—the things that show up when pressure is on and time is scarce—challenges that, if left unaddressed, can stand in the way of realizing the strategy in the given time. Without identifying these obstacles early, even the most well-planned strategies may falter.

Recognizing and addressing these growth barriers is essential for turning strategic plans into tangible results. From our work with leaders and teams across industries, it's clear that the first, and arguably the most critical, step in overcoming these obstacles is acknowledging the barriers that are present. Not fixing them just yet, but simply seeing them clearly. It is this *awareness* that provides the foundation for action.

This recognition doesn't always happen easily. In fact, many of the frustrations and inefficiencies teams face are so embedded in their daily routines that they become invisible. We often find ourselves navigating symptoms rather than addressing the underlying causes. We react to what's loud instead of looking at what's structural. As leaders, it is crucial to shed light on these hidden barriers, which may initially seem insignificant, but over time can erode productivity and team morale. These issues, small as they might appear at first, accumulate and create an environment where progress stalls.

When we engage with organizations, we consistently hear certain themes of frustration, often expressed in similar terms:

- "Meetings don't lead to decisions or action."
- "Lack of trust."
- "We operate like everything is a crisis."
- "Cross-functional relationships are strained."
- "We don't prioritize long-term success."
- "We lack commitment and follow-through."
- "Our processes get in the way of the work."

What's striking is not how different these frustrations sound, but how familiar they are. These barriers are not unique to any one company or sector—they are surprisingly common across industries. No matter the industry or organizational size, these obstacles persist, yet they often remain unspoken, accepted as the norm. We feel them, but rarely name them explicitly. We've found that most barriers to growth can be traced back to a few fundamental sources:

External Barriers

External barriers come from forces the organization can't control—shifts in the market, in regulation, in what customers actually want. For instance, the recent global pandemic had far-reaching consequences, impacting every industry and forcing organizations to rethink their strategies. Organizations must also navigate regulatory and legal factors, where fluctuating international trade tariffs, compliance requirements, or legal constraints can complicate operations. Additionally, industry trends and disruptions—whether through emerging technologies such as AI or disruptive business models—pose significant challenges.

If these external barriers are ignored, organizations risk being left behind, reacting to changes instead of anticipating them. Instead of positioning ourselves ahead of what's coming, we spend our energy responding. Companies that are unable to adapt to these external forces and don't take advantage of the opportunities that arise, risk losing their competitive edge and find themselves constantly playing catch-up.

Yet while external barriers are often visible, the internal barriers—rooted in leadership, culture, and operations—are far more insidious. They sit closer to identity and habit, quietly hindering progress without being immediately recognized.

Internal Barriers

Internal barriers often stem from leadership or organizational dynamics and can significantly impede progress. Leadership and management issues, such as unclear strategic vision, or poor decision-making, can stagnate a company's growth. These barriers frequently manifest as indecision, unclear priorities, or conflicts within teams. They rarely show up as dramatic failures; they show up as persistent frictions.

Equally, a rigid organizational culture—where adaptability is limited and communication across teams is weak—can exacerbate these challenges. Limited money, people, or technology make it even harder to execute. Even when teams recognize these issues, they often struggle to overcome them due to stronger organizational habits. This is where good intentions collide with reality.

Leaders and their teams may struggle with a lack of trust between departments or the inability to fully leverage talent, yet these problems are often rooted in the culture and management structure itself. Without addressing these cultural elements, surface-level changes will fail to yield lasting improvements. You might change the process, but the behavior stays the same.

Operational Barriers

Another common roadblock to growth is operational inefficiencies. These barriers often arise in the scalability and capacity of an organization, making it difficult to manage growth or expand into new markets. A company may have the will to grow but finds itself constrained by outdated processes, or inefficient workflows. The ambition is there, but the system can't keep up.

Inefficiencies in processes and systems, such as outdated technology or inadequate automation, can further hinder progress by draining energy and resources that could be better spent on innovation. Additionally, quality and customer satisfaction issues, whether due to poor product/service delivery or inadequate customer support, can severely impact growth and retention.

Leaders often express frustration about the time spent on these operational tasks, which ultimately leads to stagnation and hampers an organization's ability to scale efficiently. Teams spend their time fixing instead of building. This is where operational bottlenecks create real barriers to growth, forcing teams to focus on survival rather than thriving.

People-Related Barriers

Lastly, there are people-related barriers often centered around skills and talent, resistance to change, and communication and collaboration. Many organizations face challenges in attracting or retaining skilled employees, limiting their ability to grow and innovate. In a competitive talent market, these barriers can be particularly harmful, as organizations struggle to keep up with evolving skill demands. In other cases, resistance to change becomes a significant obstacle, where employees struggle with adapting to new processes or fear taking risks due to concerns about failure. These forces operate quietly, but their impact compounds over time. This creates a stagnant culture that hampers adaptability and innovation.

Additionally, poor communication and collaboration across teams or departments can further impede progress, as siloed efforts prevent cohesive growth. When departments operate in isolation, the organization's overall agility suffers. Leaders may observe a lack of accountability or commitment, but these issues are often rooted in deeper organizational structures that stifle resilience, collaboration. Again, these forces operate quietly, but their impact compounds over time. These invisible forces, which operate below the surface, can be some of the most damaging if left unaddressed.

Beliefs and Culture: The Invisible Barriers to Growth

At the root of many growth barriers are deeply held beliefs. Beliefs shape organizational culture, which in turn informs behavior. Most organizations don't struggle because of what they say they value; they struggle because of what they *actually believe*.

For example, a belief that intelligence or ability is fixed can create a Fixed Mindsets across a company, stifling innovation and encouraging risk-avoidance. The "Genius Culture," where a few are seen as "naturally gifted" and others feel unable to question leadership, is a particularly toxic barrier to growth. We've seen this play out quietly, often without anyone intending it. This type of culture not only restricts potential but also prevents employees from feeling empowered to contribute new ideas.

When beliefs go unchallenged, they become ingrained in the company's culture, making it nearly impossible to foster an environment of growth and adaptability. Leaders must start by actively examining the beliefs that underpin their teams' daily behaviors and decision-making. Not as an abstract exercise, but by paying attention close to what actually happens when pressure is on. Only by confronting these beliefs head-on can organizations begin to dismantle the barriers they create.

The Role of Beliefs in Organizational Culture

The culture of an organization, formed by shared beliefs, will either foster progress or stagnate it. Cultural inertia, driven by entrenched beliefs, can be a silent killer of growth. Recognizing the limiting beliefs within your team or company is crucial. For example: If your leadership believes that only tried-and-true methods and traditional strategies will work, you're reinforcing a "know-it-all" mindset rather than a "learn-it-all" approach. What looks like confidence is often the exact opposite: it is the fear of getting it wrong. This mindset discourages teams from taking risks and seeking out new opportunities for growth.

I've seen some transformation efforts that were incredibly successful: Generating billions, changing the way we work and live, spurring innovations and inventions. I've also seen some that ended in spectacular failure: Bankruptcies, the quiet firing of a CEO, millions in marketing poured down the drain for some new invention later swept under the rug. What struck me over time was not the quality of the strategy, but the strength of the culture behind it. The difference between these outcomes often boils down to one key factor: culture.

As Peter Drucker, the renowned management thinker and pioneer of modern business theory, famously said, "Culture eats strategy for breakfast." But what exactly shapes culture? It's not just the visible structures of leadership or the processes we follow—it's the deeply ingrained beliefs that guide how leaders and teams respond to challenges, opportunities, and change. Culture shows up in moments, not in posters.

For Satya Nadella, the CEO of Microsoft and a transformative technology leader, "The culture change [he] wanted was centered on delivering a Growth Mindset: to be customer-obsessed, diverse, and inclusive, and working as *One Microsoft* to get us there." In Nadella's case, culture was not an abstract concept, but rather a living, breathing reflection of the company's beliefs and values. What made this shift powerful was not the language, but the *consistency.*

Breaking that down, culture at Microsoft was driven by a set of beliefs—the Growth Mindset of being able to learn to work cross-siloed—which gave rise to assumptions and values like diversity and inclusion as company strengths. Working inclusively allowed every employee to learn from every other employee, which led to a specific behavior: a "customer-obsessed" approach that reflected the same desire to learn from what the customer wanted and deliver it effectively. This is a prime example of how beliefs, when nurtured properly, can create a thriving, innovative culture.

This example shows that at its core, culture is a reflection of what we believe. If you want to shift a culture, you must first address the beliefs that drive it.

Challenging Limiting Beliefs for Organizational Change

If you want to drive real change, start by naming the beliefs your organization treats as facts. When beliefs are rigid, they create invisible barriers that prevent growth. They don't announce themselves. They simply shape what feels possible.

Beliefs such as "Things have always been done this way" or that "Failure is not an option," stifle adaptation. By clinging to them, organizations limit their ability to evolve. Over time, they confuse consistency with stability.

By identifying these limiting beliefs, leaders can start diagnosing the constraints that hold their teams back. This recognition—but not action, at least not *yet*—is what sets the stage for meaningful transformation. This process begins with introspection. Leaders must look at their own beliefs and how they influence the decisions they make. The work often starts closer to home than expected.

This is crucial to understand as a RESET Leader; in order to be able to push that "reset" button on mindsets and practices whenever it's necessary to do so, a RESET Leader has to recognize that the belief is foundational to the organizational culture. Once that is part of a leader's understanding, they can RESET—at both the operational and cognitive level—first in themselves and then across the whole organization.

In other words, leaders must first transform themselves before they can transform their teams. Not by changing who they are, but by becoming aware of how they think under pressure. From there, they can help others do the same by recognizing what motivates each of us—the emotion, understanding, and satisfaction that are key to each person's sense of success.

Culture: The Mirror of Organizational Beliefs

In organizational psychology, Business Culture is defined as "a system of shared assumptions, values, and beliefs that show people what is appropriate and inappropriate behavior" (Chatman & Eunyoung, 2003[1]; Kerr & Slocum, 2005[2]). These shared institutional beliefs have a strong influence on employee behavior as well as organizational performance. They define what is considered "normal" within the

[1] Chatman, J. A., & Eunyoung Cha, S. (2003). Leading by leveraging culture. *California Management Review*, 45, 19–34.

[2] Kerr, J., & Slocum, J. W., Jr. (2005). Managing corporate culture through reward systems. *Academy of Management Executive*, 19, 130–138.

organization and dictate how employees behave. Culture ultimately answers the unspoken question: What actually gets rewarded here?

When we think about what drives organizational culture, we often focus on the visible—processes, systems, and structure. However, beneath these surface-level elements lie beliefs that quietly steer how people think, act, and engage with one another. These beliefs are the invisible threads that either hold a company together or pull it apart. They don't show up in org charts, but you can see them clearly in behavior.

The Power of a Growth Mindset in Business

Beliefs significantly impact business performance, particularly the view that intelligence is malleable, a concept popularized by Dr. Carol Dweck. The idea that intelligence and abilities can be developed is foundational to the Growth Mindset. Research shows that cognitive abilities like problem-solving and learning can be developed through experience, training, and effort. While some may see intelligence as fixed, leaders have the power to create environments that encourage learning. What they model matters more than what they say. Yet many fail to adopt this Growth Mindset.

Organizations led by Growth Mindset leaders consistently outperform their peers, demonstrating higher ethical standards, leadership effectiveness, and resilience during challenges. The difference lies in how these leaders approach their own beliefs and foster a culture of learning. They encourage experimentation, support risk-taking, and view failures as opportunities for growth. Not because failure is comfortable, but because learning matters *more* than being right.

How Beliefs Drive Leadership Effectiveness

This is where **RESET Leader** comes into play. Leaders can't just focus on changing outward behavior or policies—they must start by examining their own beliefs about growth and intelligence. What leaders believe shows up long before any policy does. If you believe that talent is fixed, that belief will infiltrate the way you lead, and the way your team approaches challenges.

Leaders who embrace a Fixed Mindset, seeing intelligence as static, often foster toxic "Genius Cultures." In companies like Enron, Kodak, and Nokia, leadership decisions went unchallenged, leading to catastrophic failures. Personality-driven leaders like Sam Bankman-Fried, Elizabeth Holmes, and Adam Neumann similarly held rigid beliefs in their own brilliance, resulting in business collapses due to their unwillingness to adapt, or willingness to bend the rules against the interests of the business. In each case, confidence—or rather, *overconfidence*—crowded out learning.

While these cases demonstrate the dangers of fixed beliefs, they also show that recognizing growth barriers isn't just about intelligence or brilliance. The true key to leadership success lies in developing a culture of continuous learning and adaptability. Leadership shifts from being the smartest person in the room to creating the conditions for learning to happen. In this context, leadership becomes less about having all the answers and more about creating an environment where everyone is encouraged to learn and grow.

As a matter of fact, psychologists who studied the "Entity" (Fixed) vs. "Incremental" (Growth) Mindsets confirm that those who believe in growth, exhibit greater motivation and performance improvements (Biddle et al., 2010[3]). Belief shapes effort, and then effort compounds over time.

From Beliefs to Action: Recognizing and Addressing Growth Barriers

Now that we've explored the relationship between beliefs and business performance, it's important to focus on the actionable steps leaders can take to recognize growth barriers from a learn-it-all mindset. This shift begins with recognizing how beliefs create growth barriers and embracing the mindset that learning never stops. Not as a slogan, but as a daily practice.

The journey to identifying growth barriers begins with examining the firmly established beliefs that guide behavior in your organization. Beliefs about intelligence and capability shape the culture and decision-making process often creating invisible barriers that limit growth. They define what feels safe to try—and what doesn't. By walking through key mindset shifts related to beliefs, leaders can systematically uncover these hidden barriers and initiate change.

[3] Biddle, S., Wang, C.K.J., Kavussanu, M., & Spray, C. (2003), Correlates of achievement goal orientations in physical activity: A systematic review of research. *European Journal of Sport Science*, 3: 1–20. https://doi.org/10.1080/17461390300073504.

From Know-It-All to Learn-It-All

As we work with leaders, one common Fixed Mindset refrain is that within their organizations "We rely on our proven track record" when formulating new missions or assessing opportunities; that is, those leaders will only take risks based on staying with what has worked in the past. What sounds like discipline often turns into avoidance. In doing so, they unintentionally create a barrier to growth. Once we put that limit in place as leaders, we have ensured that we will "Know-it-all" and, therefore, that there is nothing to learn and no way to grow because we are specifically avoiding anything new—anything from which we might learn.

To break free from this limiting belief, leaders must make a critical shift: from Know-it-all to Learn-it-all. This shift opens up the possibility of learning from every situation, not just from successes but also from challenges and failures. By embracing this Growth Mindset, leaders position themselves to recognize the barriers that are holding them back, enabling their teams to face challenges with curiosity and a readiness to adapt. Learning becomes a *responsibility,* not a risk.

Recognizing Growth Barriers Through the Learn-It-All Mindset

Understanding growth barriers requires more than just acknowledging that problems exist; it demands a shift in perspective. A Know-it-all mindset leads organizations to rely on the familiar, but a Learn-it-all mindset encourages leaders to expand their thinking, seek out new information, and continuously adapt. It replaces certainty with curiosity. This mindset is vital for recognizing the hidden barriers that often remain unnoticed until it's too late.

Let's look at a real-life example of how this mindset shift helped a leader recognize and overcome growth barriers: Brian Chesky, co-founder and CEO of Airbnb, who realized that relying solely on the familiar was limiting the company's potential. What changed was not the market itself, but what—and *how*—he chose to learn from it.

Brian Chesky and the Power of Learning

In the early days, Airbnb was just a novel idea struggling to gain traction. The founders, including Chesky, were deeply embedded in the tech startup ecosystem, which provided a certain level of insight and support. However, they soon realized that to truly innovate and scale, they needed to look beyond their immediate network. What had helped them start was no longer enough to help them grow. The limitations of their current thinking became apparent as the company sought new ways to grow.

Chesky and his co-founders made a strategic decision to diversify their network. They reached out to leaders and experts in a variety of fields unrelated directly to technology, including hospitality, design, and customer service. This wasn't about abandoning technology—it was about widening the lens. This was a deliberate effort to broaden their perspective and learn from industries that prioritize customer experience and service, areas where Airbnb wanted to excel.

Chesky's decision to live in Airbnb listings around the world was another powerful example of the Learn-it-all mindset in action. By immersing himself in the customer experience, he gained firsthand insights that led to innovations and improvements in the service Airbnb provided. Instead of relying on dashboards and reports, he chose proximity. This willingness to learn from different angles became a crucial factor in the company's growth. Chesky's openness to learning from his own product and the experiences of both hosts and guests played a critical role in Airbnb's growth, helping the company evolve beyond a tech platform into a customer-centric service that revolutionized the travel industry.

Through these interactions, Chesky shifted from a Know-it-all mindset, where the focus was solely on technological solutions, to a Learn-it-all mindset that valued diverse perspectives and holistic approaches to problem-solving. The shift wasn't dramatic—it was practical and instrumental in transforming Airbnb into a platform that prioritizes user experience for both hosts and guests.

Impact of the Mindset Shift on Recognizing Barriers

Chesky's story illustrates how shifting from a Know-it-all to a Learn-it-all mindset can help leaders recognize and break through growth barriers. This shift not only enabled Airbnb to innovate but also revealed opportunities that were previously hidden by the narrow focus on their past successes. What had once felt like certainty had become a constraint. By learning from industries they initially overlooked, Airbnb was able to expand its offerings and redefine customer service in the sharing economy.

For leaders, this shift is not just about gaining knowledge; it's about recognizing that growth barriers often stem from the belief that what worked in the past will continue to work in the future. That belief is comforting—but also dangerous. When leaders adopt a Learn-it-all mindset, they create a culture that consistently challenges the status quo. This mindset is critical for recognizing the barriers that are preventing your organization from reaching its potential.

Beliefs Create Results

To understand how deeply rooted beliefs impact growth, it's important to recognize that beliefs create your results. What we believe shapes how we think, how we make decisions, and ultimately, the actions we take. Beliefs quietly set the boundaries of what we consider possible. Leaders who believe that past successes are a reliable indicator of future growth may find themselves stuck, unable to recognize the barriers that prevent new opportunities from emerging.

On the other hand, leaders who adopt the Learn-it-all mindset are better equipped to spot these barriers. They are willing to challenge their own assumptions, and ready to pivot when necessary. They don't confuse confidence with certainty. This flexible, growth-oriented mindset helps organizations move beyond the limitations of their past and toward a future of continuous improvement and adaptability.

The Logic Chain of Belief and Action

In an organizational context, beliefs influence how decisions are made, how teams operate, and how leaders approach growth. Changing actions or behaviors without addressing the underlying beliefs is often ineffective. It treats the symptom, not the source. For leaders to recognize growth barriers and make meaningful progress, they must first shift their mindset.

By adopting the Learn-it-all mindset, leaders begin to question the assumptions that underlie their organization's behavior. They challenge the belief that past success guarantees future growth and instead focus on learning from every situation. Learning becomes a strategy, not an afterthought. This mindset shift is the first step in recognizing the barriers that are holding their organization back.

Those of us with a Growth Mindset believe that our intelligence and abilities can grow and change, so we look for ways to keep improving our approach to how we work. This mindset encourages continuous learning and adaptation, while those who have a Fixed Mindset usually end up doing a lot of posturing—which costs time and energy—or even avoiding obvious opportunities to deepen their own understanding. Avoidance often looks like expertise.

When these opportunities for growth are missed, organizations are left stagnant, and the environment can breed complacency. This avoidance of change, over time, creates a toxic Genius Culture that shuts down anyone who tries to point out problems or suggest innovation.

To the very end, these leaders—and we, as individuals—can become fixed on the idea that we are right, even when the ship is sinking and the waters rise around us. Being *right* starts to matter more than being *effective*. Sticking to what has worked in the past might feel comfortable, but it blinds us. If we remain in this Fixed Mindset, our last words will likely be, "I know best!" This dangerous level of confidence prevents the acknowledgment of blind spots, which, in turn, accelerates the decline.

This unbending belief in one's infallibility may seem harmless enough on its own, especially while the charisma of a "genius" and good initial moves are enough to keep the business growing. But when left unchecked in an organization, this overconfidence and refusal to adapt to change can spell eventual doom. Not overnight, but predictably. And while most leaders are unlikely to say they would deliberately ignore a chance to learn and grow, in many of the organizations we've worked with—both big and small—we see these mindsets deeply embedded, showing up in ways that hinder transformation.

Beliefs Shape Results

To improve your business—and to navigate challenge and change—you need to first examine the beliefs on which you and your leadership team rely. These beliefs are the hidden drivers of every action, decision, and process within an organization. Because beliefs don't just impact your results—beliefs create your results.

We can think of this as a logic chain: What we believe determines what we think and feel, which in turn determines our actions and behaviors, which ultimately determines our personal and business success. The chain always starts upstream. The chain starts with beliefs that shape how we view the world, guiding our decisions and how we respond to challenges or opportunities.

When most people want to change their results, they logically begin at the end of the chain: they try to change their actions. But changing actions alone, by brute force, is incredibly difficult, as anyone who has tried to create or break a habit knows. Actions are symptoms of deeper issues—they are influenced by underlying beliefs that, unless changed, will continue driving the same behavior. On an organizational level, trying to change actions without addressing the core beliefs is nearly impossible.

Instead, if we want to change our actions and results, we need to go all the way back up the chain and start by examining our beliefs. That's where real leverage lives. By doing so, leaders can initiate long-lasting change that permeates every level of the organization.

Changing Beliefs to Change Results

In an institutional framework, "thoughts" are institutional mindsets; "feelings" are institutional working principles, guiding—often subtly or even subconsciously—how decisions are made; "actions" are institutional practices. To boil all of that down: Change your beliefs and you will change your results. Not instantly, but sustainably. Once leaders embrace this connection, they can take intentional steps toward transforming culture and strategy.

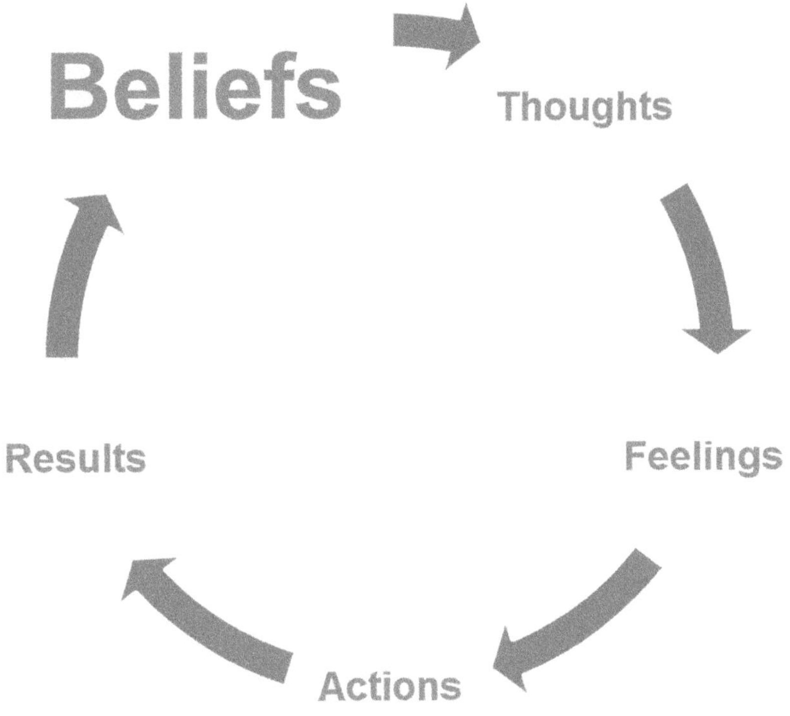

But can beliefs change? Yes. Many factors influence beliefs—new information, new experiences, and personal growth. When we learn—or have new experiences, which is a form of learning and growth—our beliefs can change.

External factors such as market shifts or technological innovations can challenge long-held assumptions, pushing us to reconsider outdated beliefs.

When someone we trust challenges us or questions our beliefs, we may examine our assumptions and change our beliefs as well. But that openness to being questioned requires humility and a commitment to growth. Beliefs are not set in stone and they can be reshaped as we gain new insights or understanding. Beliefs are fluid. They evolve as we expose ourselves to new ways of thinking.

It's also important to be open to the possibility that our beliefs may be wrong or incomplete and to be willing to revise them as new evidence or information becomes available. This can be a challenging process, but it leads to personal growth and a deeper understanding of the world. It can lead us from tradition to innovation.

But first, we have to overcome our fear of being wrong, which is the enemy of growth—and the opposite of a Growth Mindset. Growth begins the moment we loosen our grip on being right. Acknowledging our own fallibility is the first step toward embracing change.

Jackie Kegley, a philosopher known for her work in ethics, education, and American personalism, once said, "It's easier to behave your way into a new way of thinking than to think your way into a new way of behaving." This idea is key to understanding how a shift in beliefs and mindset can translate into concrete action. RESET works by creating those experiences on purpose.

I Can Learn and Develop Anything I Put My Mind To ...

Overcoming Missed Opportunities

Early in my career, I joined VanDam Machine BV, a Dutch company specializing in manufacturing printing and packaging machinery. At the time, I was responsible for sales in emerging markets like the Middle East and North Africa, which presented unique challenges due to financial constraints in these regions. Many manufacturers struggled to afford the newest manufacturing technology that more developed countries were using. However, I saw an opportunity: We could create a certified refurbishment business, offering trade-ins for existing machines and selling them at a reduced cost to emerging markets. It was a practical response to a real constraint.

While the program succeeded, I believed there was more potential. We could expand beyond refurbishing only our brand's machines and offer the service for machines from other manufacturers as well. Unfortunately, the leadership at VanDam didn't see the value in this expansion, so I left to co-found GOS International in 2000. We began mixing two business models—engineering services and trading of used equipment—allowing us to guarantee supply for refurbished machinery. This strategy helped us expand our reach and create new revenue streams. At that point, learning and adapting still felt natural.

However, when the idea of building an online marketplace came up, I hesitated. At the time, the shift to online business models was accelerating, but I was stuck in a Fixed Mindset, thinking, *We can't change into that kind of business.* Looking back, I realized that this belief—"There are some things we just can't change"—was the very barrier that held us back. Nothing external stopped us; our thinking did. Had we embraced this shift earlier, we could have positioned ourselves more competitively.

By not expanding into online trading as the industry shifted, I missed an opportunity to evolve and thrive. My reluctance to enter unknown territory was directly tied to limiting beliefs about our capacity to adapt. It was a painful lesson, but it taught me the importance of adopting the belief that I can learn and develop anything I put my mind to. The barrier wasn't skill; it was *belief.* If I had embraced this mindset earlier, I could have steered the company toward new opportunities and avoided some of the challenges that arose during the global financial crisis of 2008. In short, overcoming growth barriers isn't just about spotting opportunities—it's about having the mindset that you can adapt, learn, and grow in response to them.

How This Mindset Shift Helps Overcome Growth Barriers

Overcoming growth barriers begins with changing how you view challenges and opportunities. When leaders hold the belief that there are some things that just can't change, they limit themselves and their organizations. They stop seeking innovative solutions, and the organization becomes trapped in its current state. What once felt *realistic* becomes *restrictive*. This limits growth and creates a culture resistant to change. To overcome these barriers, leaders must shift their mindset to "I can learn and develop anything I put my mind to."

Evolving to Meet the Challenge

A clear example of how this mindset shift helps overcome growth barriers can be seen in the story of Julia Hartz, co-founder and CEO of Eventbrite. Early on, Eventbrite focused on small, local events, leveraging the platform's simplicity and flexibility. But as the company grew, the challenge of competing with larger ticketing platforms required Hartz and her team to think differently. They recognized that staying within the comfort zone of smaller events wasn't enough to scale. They needed to innovate continuously and tackle the complexities of ticketing for large-scale events. Growth demanded a different level of learning. The pivotal shift occurred when Hartz embraced the belief that her team could learn and develop the skills necessary to compete on a global scale. This mindset was crucial in Eventbrite's transformation.

Julia Hartz's story illustrates the power of a Growth Mindset in overcoming barriers. By adopting the belief that the company could adapt and evolve, Eventbrite expanded into new markets, refined its platform, and became a global leader in the ticketing industry. Had they remained locked into their original business model, they likely wouldn't have survived against much larger competitors. What changed was not ambition, but *belief*.

Stepping into the Unknown: Facing the Challenge

For many leaders, the fear of stepping into unknown territory creates the biggest growth barrier. It's easier to stick with what we know, even if it's no longer serving us. In my experience at GOS International, this reluctance to embrace the unfamiliar—such as online marketplaces—resulted in missed opportunities that could have propelled the business forward. The hesitation often comes from a lack of confidence in our ability to learn and adapt to new paradigms. We underestimate ourselves under pressure.

But the truth is, overcoming growth barriers means embracing challenges and believing that you have the capacity to learn what's needed to succeed. The key is to reframe challenges not as threats, but as invitations to learn and grow. This is where the mindset shifts from "*I can't* change" to "*I can* learn anything I put my mind to" comes into play. When leaders adopt this belief, they stop being held back by what they don't know and instead start focusing on what they can learn. Momentum follows curiosity. The potential for growth lies not in avoiding challenges but in confronting them with the confidence that, through learning, we will find the right solutions.

Growth comes from facing challenges head-on. When we avoid challenges because we feel we lack the necessary capabilities, we miss out on opportunities to grow. Overcoming growth barriers requires leaders to shift their thinking from avoiding the unknown to embracing it as a chance to develop new skills and capabilities. Discomfort becomes data. This is a key mindset shift that enables organizations to evolve beyond their current limitations and into new areas of opportunity.

When we only rest on our past achievements, we miss the "ordinary" magic of transformation. Challenges push us beyond our limits, forcing us to develop new strengths and capabilities. Leaders who believe they can learn anything they put their mind to will see challenges as opportunities, not obstacles. They stay open longer. This belief not only enhances individual growth but also sets the tone for an organization that thrives on continuous improvement.

My experience at GOS International and Julia Hartz's experience at Eventbrite both underscore the same critical lesson: A Growth Mindset is essential for overcoming barriers and driving innovation. The belief that you can learn and develop anything you need to succeed enables leaders to break through their limitations and lead their organizations toward new growth. In both cases, the shift from "This is how things are" to "We can learn and change" unlocked new avenues for growth.

Leaders who adopt this mindset will be better equipped to face challenges, knowing that their success doesn't depend on their current capabilities, but on their willingness to learn and adapt. Overcoming growth barriers is not about having all the answers from the start—it's about being willing to learn and grow through the process. That *willingness* is what separates *survival* from *progress*. This mindset is what differentiates companies that survive from those that thrive in times of change.

Where Are You in the Game?

Before we look at a list of the Fixed Mindsets, I want to take a moment and think of a game. You might be a fan of baseball, basketball, ice hockey, soccer, or any other team sport—they all offer the same schema for us to consider.

Now think of the stadium—you see an audience in the stands. On the sidelines of the field, you see the technical staff and coaches; and, finally, of course, you see the players on the field. The question is, where are you in this structure? And just as important—how did you end up here?

- Are you in the audience cheering on the players and coaches, adding energy and enthusiasm for the effort?
- Are you coaching—planning out the strategy and watching over the execution, offering perspective to those really in the thick of it?
- Or are you on the field and playing—grappling with the details, the negotiations, drawing insight from coaches and energy from the roaring crowd at crucial moments?

And wherever you are, is this the place you want to be? Is this your desired role? Your efforts should align with your desired role. Obviously, they should also align with your talents and the needs of the team! Misalignment shows up as frustration long before it shows up in results. But let's stay, for a moment, with the central actor in this scenario: you. If you are already in the role you desire, then putting in effort is easier (though perhaps not simple); if you are finding that you want to change roles, moving from player to coach or audience to player, then the difficulty is magnified. How many of us have been excited about a promotion only to then learn how much we had to learn in our new role?

In either case, you start with recognizing what holds you back from putting in your best effort—what are the current behaviors that no longer help you find the role you really want and what are the underlying mindsets that cause that behavior? This is where growth becomes personal.

Be the Change You Want to See in Others

As leaders, it's easy to expect our teams to adapt, evolve, and overcome challenges, but we often forget that real transformation starts with us. If we want our teams to recognize and address growth barriers, we must first model the behaviors and mindsets we want to see in them. This first step in the RESET framework—recognizing growth barriers—isn't just about identifying obstacles in others; it's about holding ourselves accountable for the changes we need to make as leaders. Leadership always goes first. We can't expect our teams to grow if we aren't willing to grow first.

Leadership transformation doesn't begin with grand, sweeping organizational shifts; it begins with the willingness to look inward. To recognize and remove the barriers that hinder progress, we must first acknowledge our role in maintaining them. When we adopt the belief "They will never change," we reinforce the very barriers we are trying to dismantle. This passive attitude towards change stifles progress. However, by shifting to a mindset of "Be the change you want to see in others," we empower ourselves to lead by example. Change becomes *embodied*, not *instructed*. This shift encourages leaders to take responsibility for the changes they wish to see, creating a ripple effect throughout the organization.

This shift is crucial. It forces leaders to stop waiting for external circumstances or others to change and instead focus on transforming their own mindset and behaviors. In doing so, they become the catalyst for broader organizational transformation. When leaders embrace the mindset of being the change, they signal to their teams that transformation is not just an organizational mandate but a personal commitment to growth and adaptation. People follow what they see practiced. This kind of leadership inspires others to do the same.

Overcoming Growth Barriers: From Recognition to Action

Recognizing growth barriers is only the beginning. Once these barriers are identified, the next step is to overcome them—and this requires more than just recognition; it requires action. This is where the mindset shift from "They will never change" to "Be the change you want to see in others" becomes essential. It bridges the gap between awareness and action. Insight only matters if it leads to *movement*. This shift prepares leaders to dive deeper into the specific mindset shifts that will help them overcome these barriers at every level of the organization. It's not enough to see the obstacles; leaders must actively work to remove them.

In the next chapter, we will explore the mindset shifts that leaders must embrace to not only recognize but also overcome growth barriers. These shifts will challenge long-standing assumptions, change how we approach challenges, and unlock the full potential of both leaders and teams. Each of these mindset shifts is a tool to push beyond the status quo and create new pathways for success.

Remember, the transformation you want to see in your organization begins with you. As we move forward, you'll learn how adopting these specific mindset shifts will help you lead your team through the process of breaking down barriers and unlocking new opportunities for growth. By embodying the change you wish to see, you become the driver of a more adaptive, and successful organization.

Scan the QR codes below to access short RESET Leader videos that help you recognize growth barriers, shift mindsets, and experiment with new habits.

Growth Area: Beliefs

Explore how your beliefs about intelligence and ability shape how you learn, adapt, and grow—and how to shift limiting mindsets.

https://qr.resetleader.com/MUXcxVzj

CHAPTER THREE

Evaluate Mindset Shifts

The Lens that Shapes Our World

Our actions are not random; they are the direct result of how we interpret the world around us. Everything we do—every decision, every reaction—runs through a filter we rarely examine. That filter is mindset. Mindsets are the mental lenses through which we view ourselves, others, and the situations we face. They are the filters that shape how we see situations, how we feel about them, and how we behave in response. In simple terms: our mindsets shape our world—and how we move through it.

These mental lenses don't just influence what we perceive; they also determine how we act. A leader who views challenges as obstacles to be avoided will act very differently from one who sees them as opportunities for growth. Similarly, a team member who views feedback as a threat to their competence will approach it far differently than someone who sees it as a tool for improvement. The mindset shapes the behavior, which in turn shapes the results. That's why strategy can be clear and execution can still be too slow or stall.

Think of mindsets as the operating system running in the background of your organization. Just as a computer's operating system dictates how it processes data, mindsets drive how individuals and teams process information, solve problems, and collaborate. If the operating system is rigid or outdated, it limits adaptability and growth. Conversely, a flexible and growth-oriented operating system allows for innovation and resilience, even in the face of challenges.

Understanding these mental lenses is the first step in recognizing the patterns that shape behavior. By evaluating and evolving our mindsets, we open the door to intentional, transformative action—both as individuals and as leaders. Not by forcing new behavior, but by updating what drives it.

If It Doesn't Challenge You, It Doesn't Change You

Picture this: You're thinking through your past achievements. It's like looking at old photos of times when things felt aligned—when you were effective, confident, in flow. It feels good to pause there. Familiar and affirming.

But when we stay there—resting on past wins—we quietly trade movement for comfort. And that's where growth stops. Comfort can be a trap. Not because it's wrong, but because it removes the tension that change requires. Real growth usually feels inconvenient, not exhilarating. True growth happens when we bravely step away from the comforts of past successes and move toward an unknown future.

Another reason why we may prefer to rest on past achievements is because we seek external validation for those past achievements before we can move forward and onto the next challenge. It is like relying on a constantly changing weather forecast to know when we are ready to step outside. It's us who make it happen; the weather is just the set of external circumstances. Similarly, it's us who can validate our work. It's time to switch gears—to Reset—and seek that validation from within. That's where maturity in leadership starts. Embrace the power of our own judgment in all we've achieved and trust that we are capable of achieving greatness, even in the face of challenges. In reality, we are capable because of those challenges and all we've learned through them.

Evolving to Compete

Returning to the example of Eventbrite we discussed in the previous chapter: When Julia Hartz and her team entered a market dominated by larger, more established ticketing services, they initially focused on small events and leveraged their platform's ease of use and flexibility. But the Fixed Mindset of resting on these early achievements was not Hartz's style. This shift mattered—not because what worked was wrong, but because staying there would have capped what was possible. This *mindset shift* was crucial to Eventbrite as it propelled its evolution from a service focused on small local events to a global ticketing platform. They didn't abandon what worked—they stopped letting it limit them.

Rather than a story of resting on early successes, Julia Hartz's story of significant growth and positive change highlights the importance of persistence, and the continuous pursuit of improvement—principles that resonate with entrepreneurs and leaders across industries. It's a simple pattern: learn fast, adjust, and repeat.

Each challenge has learning potential; each is an invitation to transform our mindset and embrace the challenge as a catalyst for change that can propel us toward new horizons. Every challenge asks the same question: will you protect your identity, or will you learn? When we leap into those new realms, we ignite our creativity, and unlock a world of possibilities.

I experienced this myself. I had convinced myself that my age defined my physical limits. It wasn't until I re-evaluated this belief that I took action, starting with a single, humbling run to the end of my street.

Envisioning a Future-You

Our mindsets are powerful, not just in shaping how we approach challenges but also in how we envision our potential. One way to unlock this potential is to connect with a vision of your **Future-You**—the person you aspire to become. **Future-You** isn't an abstract idea; it's a version of yourself that exists in possibility, shaped by the actions you take today.

I learned this firsthand through a deeply personal challenge. I grew up playing soccer and doing martial arts, but this faded away once I started my professional career.

By early 2007, a decade into my career, playing with my young children in the backyard left me out of breath. I knew they were only getting more active, so if I wanted to play with them as they grew, I would need to up my own game. I reframed my wish that I was able to play longer with them into a vision. I was able to see the Future-me, one who could play a soccer game with my kids without giving up after ten minutes, not as a distant dream but as someone I could work toward becoming. Now that I had the belief that this Future-me could exist, how would I get there?

After looking for a sport that fit my schedule, I decided on running. My first run lasted twelve minutes—all the way to the end of the street—and I was completely spent. After one week, however, I felt strong enough to run a few minutes longer, and within a month, I could run for twenty minutes without any stops.

At first I found it boring, but the more I learned, the more I enjoyed it. I saw change not just in my body, but in my ability to learn something new. I was becoming something more than Present-me; I was, therefore, capable of becoming Future-me. Running without technical knowledge invites injuries, so I researched different programs and looked for coaches to guide me. This helped me challenge myself both mentally and physically. It also brought me into community with others tackling similar challenges for different reasons and with widely varying approaches; this was a new pool of people who affirmed my Growth Mindset and my transformation. Together, we pushed each other toward who we were becoming.

When my cousin suggested entering the New York City Marathon the following year, my Future-me vision foundered; it sounded impossible. The idea of suffering more than 5km felt already too much, and 42km seemed absolutely ridiculous! But I rose to the challenge by taking small steps, relying on my community, learning how to train in both mind and body for that particular set of stresses, charting progress, and forgiving setbacks. I ran my first NYC marathon in 2007 and have since run two others. The Future-me is now the Present-me.

The Trap of Belief: How Mindsets Shape Behavior

The power of mindsets lies in how they shape the choices we make and the actions we take. They influence everything from how we approach challenges to how we perceive the success of others. These mental lenses, which are naturally formed to help us navigate complexity, determine how we interpret and respond to the situations we encounter daily.

As leaders, the stakes are higher: Your mindset not only guides your own choices but also shapes the culture around you. That's why it matters to pause and examine the two lenses—Fixed and Growth Mindsets—that so often determine whether you stay stuck or move forward. When pressure rises, the default lens wins.

Before we delve into Fixed and Growth Mindsets, it's important to recognize a deeper challenge—one that isn't often discussed. Many leaders face the isolating experience of bearing ultimate responsibility, which can create blind spots in how we evaluate our own mindsets.

The Leadership Challenge No One Talks About

Many executives feel the loneliness of being a leader. It is a unique experience. As leaders, we often bear the weight of important decisions, the responsibility for the well-being of our teams or organizations, and the need to maintain a strong image. This can create a sense of isolation, where you may feel that there are few people who truly understand the pressures and complexities of your role. It's not just lonely; it can quietly reinforce the belief that you have to be the one who knows.

And, sure, the CEO is The Leader, so they may experience this isolation most intensely. At the same time, if you're a division leader or a team leader, you may recognize your own version of this loneliness. One of the flipsides of being a leader—of being valued for your drive and your vision and your ability to enroll others in the larger effort—is that, on some division-based or team-based level, the buck stops with you.

And while leaders often have a network of colleagues and advisors, there may still be moments when you feel unable to fully share your concerns, fears, or doubts with others. The constant need to project strength and confidence can make it difficult to show vulnerability or admit to personal struggles. Additionally, the higher you rise in leadership positions, the fewer peers or equals you may have, which can further contribute to a sense of loneliness. There may be a scarcity of individuals who can relate to your specific challenges, experiences, and decision-making responsibilities. So you carry it, quietly.

The loneliness of the CEO may actually set up a negative feedback loop within the organization: a mindset culture of isolation. Sustained loneliness at the top is not, however, an inevitable consequence of leadership. There are ways to manage this challenge: Many leaders actively cultivate support networks, seek mentorship, and engage in peer communities to mitigate this feeling. Opening up to trusted individuals and finding ways to connect with others in similar positions—being the RESET Leader in the sense of knowing you need a new way forward—can help alleviate this challenge and provide valuable perspectives. The shift is simple: from "only I can" to "I don't have to carry this alone." At the same time, realizing and articulating that loneliness is a transformational stretch exercise—a difficult reflection on yourself by yourself—and that the camaraderie of the team can help carry the load, all of that puts you in the position of modeling deep new mindsets and practices.

Which is to say that once you recognize isolation as a growth barrier—a mindset related to how you meet challenges—then you can start to think of the mindset shifts needed to leap over that barrier. CEOs may be running the biggest most influential companies, and yet it's important to also realize there is still stuff we don't know—there are still ways in which we can grow. Realizing that is the first step toward putting down the weight that the "only I can" isolation imposes. It's time to step back for a moment, to embrace the neuroscience of the Growth Mindset, and to take your leadership to the next level.

And then it's crucial to recognize that the essence of overcoming obstacles transcends hierarchical levels.

The journey from shifting mindsets is not reserved for the upper echelons of corporate leadership alone; it is a universal path that individuals at all levels can navigate and benefit from. Much like the CEO, division leader, or team leader who grapples with the loneliness of leadership and the pressure of decision-making, professionals across the spectrum encounter their own versions of these challenges. Whether it's the fear of failure, resistance to change, or the struggle to adapt to new roles and responsibilities, the underlying principles apply universally.

This shared struggle serves as a powerful reminder that the process of personal and professional development is interconnected, transcending individual roles within an organization. By acknowledging the commonality of these experiences, you can foster a more inclusive environment that encourages dialogue, and a collective pursuit of growth. It is through this lens that we can begin to see the transformational power of shifting from a Fixed Mindset—where certain beliefs become rigid under pressure—to a Growth Mindset, which embraces them as opportunities for development.

And seeing you model openness in the face of challenges, and growth in the face of risk, helps to broaden each person's understanding of what leadership looks like. This modeling of mindset shifts is critical because it highlights the foundational role that mindsets play in shaping not just individual actions but the culture and dynamics of entire teams. By understanding how these mental frameworks influence behavior, we can begin to identify the patterns that drive or hinder progress.

As we delve together into the specific Fixed Mindsets prevalent across all levels of many organizations, we'll explore how you can cultivate a growth-oriented approach, enabling you to not only navigate but thrive amidst the challenges you face.

But overcoming the isolation of leadership requires more than just external support: It calls for an internal shift, one rooted in the courage to embrace vulnerability.

Leading with Open Hands

The loneliness of being a leader is a unique challenge that often stems from the fear of exposing vulnerabilities. Similarly, many mindsets arise from this same fear. But in reality, as we've explored, our vulnerability is a power. Since each of us is innately vulnerable, the acknowledgement of our particular vulnerabilities is connective—it binds us together at our most human level.

The journey through challenges is not solitary. It involves recognizing that our vulnerabilities are not weaknesses but gateways to growth. As demonstrated through the stories of visionary leaders and the practices that foster collective resilience, we see that challenges are not merely obstacles but opportunities that invite us to grow, innovate, and transform.

By fostering an environment where seeking help is celebrated as a strength, you create a culture that not only supports individual advancement but also propels the entire organization forward. This culture of mutual support and resilience equips you to tackle higher stakes and more complex challenges, ensuring that with each hurdle crossed, you not only meet your goals but exceed them, setting new benchmarks for success.

As leaders, embracing the mindset shift—from viewing challenges as threats to seeing them as opportunities—enables you to lead by example. It signals to your teams that growth is a practice, not a milestone. Let's carry this forward—showing up honestly with each other, and treating every challenge as a chance to grow together.

When you learn from wins and setbacks alike, growth becomes something you build together—not something that happens to you.

The Bigger the Challenge ... The More Rewarding the Opportunity

One inspiring real-life story that embodies the essence of seeing big challenges as rewarding opportunities comes from the journey of Arunachalam Muruganantham, an inventor and social entrepreneur from a small village in India. His story is not just about innovation but about choosing learning over comfort and challenging deeply rooted social norms and taboos surrounding menstrual health.

Muruganantham observed his wife using old rags during her menstrual cycle because sanitary pads were too expensive. Concerned for her health and hygiene, he embarked on a quest to develop an affordable solution for menstrual hygiene management. Despite having no experience in materials engineering or manufacturing, he dedicated himself to creating a low-cost sanitary pad. He didn't start with expertise. He started with care and curiosity.

The challenge was immense. Not only did he lack the technical knowledge, but he also faced social ostracism. His community shunned him and his family questioned his actions, unable to understand his obsession with creating sanitary pads. Muruganantham, however, was undeterred. He saw beyond the immediate technical challenge to the larger social issue at stake: improving women's health and empowering them through better hygiene. He stayed with the problem longer than most people were willing to tolerate the discomfort.

Through years of iteration, testing, and learning from each setback, Muruganantham finally developed a simple machine that could produce low-cost sanitary pads. His invention has not only provided access to sanitary products for millions of women in India and other countries—it has also broken taboos around menstruation, promoting more open discussions about women's health. Progress didn't come from getting it right quickly, but from refusing to stop learning.

Muruganantham's story is a testament to the Growth Mindset. He approached an enormous challenge with the belief that learning and persistence would lead to progress. His journey wasn't about heroic effort or endless sacrifice; it was about persevering when the outcome was still uncertain. This story illustrates that facing big challenges head-on, with a focus on learning and adaptation, can lead to extraordinary achievements and impact far beyond the initial goal.

Muruganantham, known as the "Menstrual Man," has become a symbol of innovation and social change, proving that embracing challenges is indeed the fastest way to move a project forward, grow as a leader, and make a significant difference in the world. Not because the challenge is big—but because learning rises to meet it.

Rising to the Challenge Means Leveling Up

Some team members tend to give up too easily and avoid seeking support from others as a way of staying on course toward shared goals. One reason is a lack of awareness of what seeking support actually offers. It goes far beyond hitting a milestone or solving a short-term problem. Support brings perspective, and learning—often exactly when clarity is hardest to access alone. By not involving others, people miss out on encouragement and the collective intelligence around them.

Another reason team members avoid seeking support is the fear of vulnerability. Asking for help or support can make people feel exposed; they may worry about being judged or seen as incompetent—worries that are based on a false belief that each person should know enough, be enough, to achieve every goal. This belief quietly works against growth. This fear hampers their willingness to seek assistance. And that, in turn, can cause them to doubt their own instincts and even give up without reaching their goal (or their own potential).

Encouraging a supportive and nonjudgmental work environment helps individuals overcome this fear. When asking for help is normalized as a sign of awareness rather than weakness, teams unlock a different level of performance. Collaboration stops being transactional and becomes developmental. People don't just solve problems together—they *grow* through them.

I've seen this dynamic powerfully illustrated in the transformation of Barry-Wehmiller, a global supplier of manufacturing technology and services, under the leadership of CEO Bob Chapman.

When Bob Chapman took over as CEO in the late 1970s, he faced the immense challenge of transforming Barry-Wehmiller from a struggling equipment company into a thriving enterprise. His approach was unique in that he focused intensely on the company's culture and the well-being of his employees. He introduced the principle of "Truly Human Leadership," which emphasizes caring for employees so that they feel valued and trusted. This wasn't a soft idea—it was a *strategic choice* about how growth actually happens.

Chapman stabilized the company and then began making it thrive, a journey that unfolded over decades. Even after facing thirty years of challenging times, he wasn't finished learning; one of the key challenges he encountered during this period was the 2008 financial crisis, a period when many companies were laying off workers. Instead of layoffs, still true to its Truly Human Leadership culture, Barry-Wehmiller implemented a program of shared sacrifice. Employees were required to take unpaid leave, and it was positioned not as a cutback but as a collective effort to help each other through hard times. This approach not only saved jobs but also fostered a strong sense of community and mutual support among employees.

This environment encouraged employees to rise together when facing challenges. The result was not just the company's survival through a tough economic period but significant growth for Barry-Wehmiller and a renewed wave of innovation. Employees became more engaged, contributing to improvements and new ideas because they knew they had the support of the organization—*and* the support of their peers. Rising to the challenge together became a shared capability, not an individual burden.

This strategy was not just a survival tactic but a transformative shift toward collective resilience. Chapman's leadership emphasized the importance of each team member's contribution to the greater good and nurtured a culture where asking for help and supporting each other were seen as strengths. The approach helped employees not only to navigate the crisis together but also to emerge stronger, with deeper trust and ownership in the organization's future, strengthening their commitment to the company's values.

Barry-Wehmiller not only survived the crisis but thrived, showcasing how rising to challenges as a unified workforce can fundamentally level up an organization's capacity for resilience and innovation. The lesson is clear: when leadership creates the conditions for people to support one another, growth accelerates—especially when the stakes are high.

Fixed and Growth Mindsets: A Framework for Evaluation

Building on Dweck's research, mindsets can be categorized into two broad perspectives: Fixed Mindsets and Growth Mindsets. Each represents a distinct way of thinking that shows up in different behaviors and approaches to life and work.

- Fixed Mindsets: These are grounded in the belief that abilities, intelligence, and talents are static. People with a Fixed Mindset often focus on proving their competence, avoiding situations that might reveal a weakness. The underlying question is often: "How do I not look bad?" This perspective can lead to risk aversion, resistance to feedback, and a tendency to view challenges as threats rather than opportunities.
- Growth Mindsets: By contrast, Growth Mindsets are based on the belief that abilities can be developed through effort, learning, and persistence. Those with a Growth Mindset approach challenges with curiosity, embrace feedback as a chance to improve, and see the success of others as a source of inspiration and learning. The question shifts to: "What can I learn here?"

While these two categories represent opposite ends of a spectrum, most of us exhibit a mix of both mindsets, depending on the situation. Mindsets are contextual, not labels. The key is learning to recognize when a Fixed Mindset might be holding you back and how to cultivate a Growth Mindset in its place.

The Impact of Lenses on Leadership and Team Dynamics

As leaders, understanding the lenses through which you view your work, your team, and yourself is critical. These mental lenses shape how you perceive challenges, and even the success of others. Do you see challenges as insurmountable roadblocks or as invitations to grow? Do you view the success of others as a threat to your position, or as a signpost for what's possible? These are not theoretical questions. They show up *every day* in leadership behavior.

A leader's mindset doesn't just influence their own behavior; it cascades throughout the organization. If a leader views challenges as opportunities to learn and grow, this mindset creates a culture of experimentation, collaboration, and resilience. Conversely, a Fixed Mindset at the top can lead to risk aversion, blame-shifting, and stagnation. What leaders tolerate—and model—quickly becomes the norm.

However, evaluating mindsets is not always straightforward. Certain entrenched mindsets act as barriers to progress, making it difficult to recognize or address underlying issues. Some common mindsets while working with leaders or teams we've observed include:

- **"We operate like everything is a crisis":** Constantly reacting rather than planning creates a cycle of chaos and prevents meaningful progress.
- **"We don't embrace discomfort and challenge":** Avoiding discomfort stifles growth and keeps teams stuck in their comfort zones.

- **"Our purpose is unclear":** A lack of clarity in purpose leads to misaligned goals and scattered efforts.
- **"No alignment on strategic priorities":** Without shared priorities, teams pull in different directions, slowing progress.
- **"Outdated tech tools":** Clinging to obsolete tools and processes limits innovation and efficiency.
- **"We use good (or bad) results as an excuse not to change":** Success can breed complacency, while failure often fosters fear, both of which block improvement.
- **"Lack of forward thinking—we miss staying ahead of trends":** Teams that don't anticipate future changes risk becoming irrelevant.
- **"We fail to identify the critical tasks":** A focus on low-impact activities rather than strategic priorities drains energy and resources.

These mindsets are often so ingrained that they feel like "just the way things are," which is precisely what makes them hard to spot. What feels normal is often the clearest signal of an unexamined mindset. Recognizing them is the first step toward shifting the lens.

The first step to evaluating mindset movement is recognizing the lens you're currently looking through. Mindsets are not static; they can shift and evolve. By identifying and addressing the Fixed Mindsets that may be holding you or your team back, you create the space for adaptability, and growth.

Recognizing and evaluating our mindsets isn't just about understanding where we stand; it's about paving the way for meaningful shifts. Each mindset—whether fixed or growth—shapes the decisions we make and the cultures we create. The journey of evaluating mindsets prepares us for the deeper work of shifting them. In the next section, we'll explore how these shifts can transform not only our approach to challenges but also how we view and support the success of others.

Making the Shift

So how do we make this shift? How do we get over our hardwired pull toward immediate gratification and instead lean into the challenges in a way that will bring long-term health and growth?

In the early days of my entrepreneurial career, I cofounded a tech venture and faced a significant challenge: I was ready to ship a production machine to a client's facility, a large packaging firm in Denmark, only to discover it still had many performance errors. This situation became a prime battleground between my mindsets.

My Fixed Mindset rushed out, almost panicking. Initially, the looming errors triggered a wave of anxiety. The self-doubt yelled, "What if we can't fix it? What if the client loses trust?" This fear of failure, intensified by my non-engineering background, tempted me to postpone the shipment, to avoid the risk—a classic response from a Fixed Mindset trying to stay safe.

Recognizing the trap of my Fixed Mindset helped me consciously pivot to a Growth Mindset. Despite the machine's errors, we decided to ship it, transparently communicating the situation to the client. That was the shift: instead of hiding, we collaborated. Working closely with the client and my team, we tackled the performance issues head-on, turning a potential crisis into an opportunity to reach our goals.

Shipping the machine with errors and fixing them over the following months as it was taken into production was a real-life lesson in resilience and growth. No matter how well we might have engineered the machine, the fact is that it was only in a real-life production environment that we were able to see the problems. That part was inevitable, so it was better to have just gotten to that point of learning and problem-solving earlier than later. The Build—Measure—Learn cycle, more on that later, became real, and Failure became *learning.*

This experience taught me that embracing challenges—and sometimes, the imperfections that come with them—can lead to greater learning opportunities and stronger relationships with clients. It proved that success is not about perfection from the outset but about staying in the game long enough to learn what reality is asking you.

Mindsets Can Be Measured

For too long, mindsets have been seen as abstract concepts, difficult to pin down, and even harder to act upon. But the truth is, mindsets are not intangible; they can be observed, understood, and measured. The language we use is one of the most powerful indicators of our mindset. It reflects how we interpret challenges, and change.

Let's make this tangible because mindset can often feel fluffy. This is where language becomes critical. Our words often act as a mirror to our mindsets. For instance, when faced with change, do we instinctively call it a "problem," or do we frame it as an "opportunity"? That subtle difference in language can profoundly impact how we approach the situation and whether we shut down or stay open.

The Mindset Language Barrier

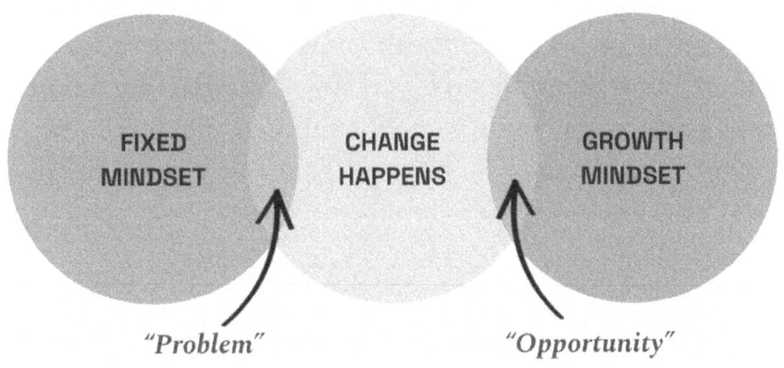

Your mindset influences your language, and your language influences your mindset. Choose your words carefully.

When change happens, the language we choose—"problem" versus "opportunity"—does more than describe the situation; it shapes our approach and reinforces our underlying mindset. Your mindset influences your language, and your language, in turn, influences your mindset. Choosing words carefully is a crucial step if we want to measure what's really going on and shift it on purpose.

To help leaders and teams go beyond the abstract and make their mindsets tangible, we've developed the **8Star Mindset Assessment** specifically for evaluating mindsets across eight growth areas. This tool is designed to move from language to action, helping identify specific areas where Fixed and Growth Mindsets show up. It makes mindsets concrete by providing clear, actionable insights across eight key areas, guiding individuals and organizations in their journey toward greater adaptability and innovation.

For teams, the **TeamStar Report** extends this framework, offering insights into collective mindsets and behaviors. It's one thing to shift your own mindset; it's another to align an entire team toward a culture of growth. As we explore how mindsets influence behavior in this chapter, we'll also uncover practical ways to use tools like these to create meaningful change in your organization.

8Star Mindset Assessment

Understanding how mindsets shape behavior is the first step, but true transformation requires specificity. That's where the **8Star Mindset Assessment** becomes a vital tool. It breaks down the broad concept of mindset into eight distinct growth areas, each representing a crucial aspect of how we think, and behave at work.

These growth areas are more than abstract ideas—they are measurable, actionable, and reflective of real-world behaviors. They help individuals and teams identify where Fixed Mindsets might be holding them back and where Growth Mindsets can unlock potential. By focusing on these areas, leaders gain clarity on what's working, what needs to change, and how to align their mindset with their missions.

Let's zoom in on a few critical areas that illustrate how powerful and subtle shifts in mindset can transform how we lead, and collaborate. These aren't just personal insights; they are levers for unlocking potential, and driving real organizational change.

Shifting from a Fixed to a Growth Mindset is not a one-time revelation. It is an ongoing process of recognizing and evaluating. There are also misperceptions about Growth Mindsets, often oversimplified into "Think positive and try hard." But real change goes deeper. It requires leaders and teams to develop a shared language around how mindset shows up in everyday work, especially when urgency strikes, pressure increases, or we feel triggered.

Building on Dweck's foundational research, we've found in our work with leaders, from startups to global enterprises, that Growth Mindset barriers consistently surface across eight recurring areas:

- **Beliefs** about Intelligence
- Openness to **Risktaking**
- How we respond to **Challenges**
- Our views on **Effort**
- How we perceive the **Successes of Others**
- Our openness to **Feedback**

- Learning from **Failure**
- Our level of **Persistence**

These are not isolated traits, but they are windows into how we interpret the world and operate within it.

How These Growth Areas Guide Action

These eight areas provide a roadmap for evaluating and transforming mindsets at both individual and organizational levels. By examining specific behaviors in each area, you can identify where Fixed Mindsets are holding back progress and take targeted steps toward fostering a Growth Mindset. The 8Star Mindset Assessment helps make these shifts tangible, offering actionable insights and pathways for growth, both individually and as teams.

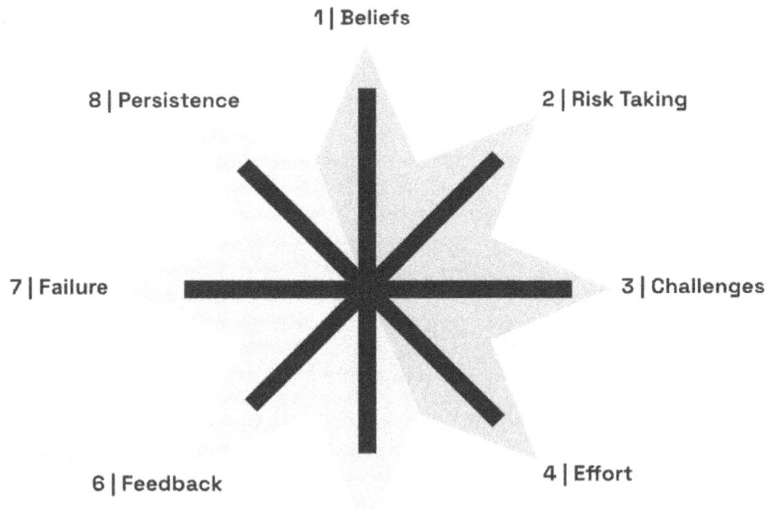

Mindset Mission: Shifting Perspectives on Success and Challenges

We hear, see, and read them everywhere: success stories of people who have broken a record, developed a phenomenal invention, or had an outstanding career milestone. Some write bestselling books about their successes or have their stories become blockbuster movies. And they reach a large audience because those stories inspire and motivate us.

Inspirational books and movies can be encouraging because they provide us with a sense of hope about the possibility of achieving our own goals. They often tell the story of someone who has overcome obstacles to achieve success, which can serve as a reminder that it is possible for us to do the same. Additionally, they can provide practical advice and strategies for achieving one's goals. The messages and stories in these books and movies often inspire people to take action and make positive changes in their own lives.

Unfortunately, that is not always the result. Or not the only result. The success of others can also feel overwhelming and discouraging. This discouragement is often caused by social comparison, which occurs when we evaluate our own self-worth based on the success of others. For example, anxiety may strike before a school reunion if you feel inadequate or insecure about your own accomplishments in comparison to those of your former classmates. Or, as you are scrolling through social media, you may begin to feel bad about your own personal life or career in the face of so many happy pictures of acquaintances.

Others' successes in our workplace can have this discouraging effect as well. We've all experienced it: When a colleague gets a promotion because they successfully completed a project that we thought wasn't that impressive, or when we apply for a position, but another colleague gets the job. Even if you feel they will do a great job, it can still sting.

The successes of others can make us feel inadequate, emphasize that we have not achieved certain goals, or remind us of our own failures. That comparison can then lead to negative emotions, such as jealousy or envy, which further discourage us. There's a RESET needed here, for sure, so let's dig into what's happening.

Comparing ourselves to others creates an unrealistic standard of success. We often focus on the strengths and accomplishments of others and ignore their struggles. Conversely, we focus on our failures and ignore our strengths, in part because our strengths are normal to us; they seem terrifically unimpressive solely because they are ours. When we compare our behind-the-scenes struggles to their highlight reel of successes, our own struggles feel more significant and overwhelming. Social media and other forms of media can exacerbate this problem because we are all showcasing a curated version of our lives to some extent. All of this makes it easy to feel like everyone else is doing better than we are.

And here's the deeper mindset problem. In her research, Dweck found that those who feel threatened by the success of others also tend to avoid challenges, see effort as ultimately pointless, and focus on "looking smart." So when we're in this spiral, we limit ourselves to things that we know we can do well.

This mindset problem not only affects individuals but can also have significant implications for organizational dynamics. A Fixed Mindset in response to the success of others often leads to the creation or reinforcement of silos within an organization. When employees feel threatened by their colleagues' achievements, they may become reluctant to share information, collaborate, or seek help, fearing that doing so will highlight their own perceived inadequacies. This protective behavior stifles innovation and hampers the organization's overall growth.

On the other hand, fostering a strong Growth Mindset encourages employees to view their colleagues' successes as opportunities for learning and development. In such an environment, cross-departmental collaborations thrive, and knowledge-sharing becomes the norm. Teams are more likely to leverage diverse skills and perspectives, and create a culture of continuous learning. By embracing a Growth Mindset, organizations can break down silos, promote teamwork, and unlock their full potential.

The Challenge of Shifting Mindsets

But what happens when these insights meet resistance? Recognizing the negative feelings that arise in the face of others' success is just the first step. Shifting those feelings into opportunities for growth often requires confronting powerful patterns of thought and behavior. This is where the real challenge emerges.

A Fixed Mindset is rarely limited to how we perceive others' achievements; it also impacts how we approach challenges. Just as some feel discouraged by success stories, others find themselves avoiding new opportunities altogether, fearing failure or judgment. The same spiral that inhibits collaboration in teams can prevent individuals and organizations from taking the necessary steps toward growth.

To embrace a Growth Mindset in these moments requires deliberate effort and a willingness to lean into discomfort. We must move from avoidance to action, from seeing challenges as threats to recognizing them as opportunities to learn and grow. This shift can be daunting, but it is the key to unlocking personal and organizational potential.

In the next section, we'll explore the mindset shifts that are crucial for overcoming these challenges. What follows are the shifts that matter most—and they're harder than they seem.

The Power of Mindset Shifts in Overcoming Challenges

It's important to remember that success is not a destination; it's a journey. And there is always room for growth and development; in fact, growth and development are the truest measures of success on that journey. By studying the success of others and learning from them, we can improve our own skills and knowledge and move closer to achieving our own goals.

However, this journey is often hindered by Fixed Mindsets that create barriers to collaboration, and trust. As we explore the challenges involved in shifting mindsets, let's delve into three pivotal mindset shifts that have enabled transformative growth and success in both individuals and organizations.

From "We Are Lone Wolves" to "We're in It Together"

A compelling example of this transformation is the cultural shift at Microsoft under CEO Satya Nadella. When Nadella assumed leadership in 2014, the company's culture was siloed, with departments often operating in isolation or even competition. This Fixed Mindset stifled collaboration, innovation, and growth. Recognizing this, Nadella championed a Growth Mindset across the organization, starting with the critical mindset shift from "We are lone wolves" to "We're in it together."

Nadella emphasized empathy, learning, and collaboration as the cornerstones of Microsoft's culture. He introduced changes that encouraged cross-departmental projects and open communication. For example, the integration of LinkedIn with Microsoft products like Office 365 and Dynamics exemplified the power of collaboration. Employees began to understand that their colleagues' successes could contribute to their own growth and that shared achievements would ultimately drive the company's broader goals. This mindset shift not only improved interdepartmental relationships but also boosted overall company performance, transforming Microsoft into a cohesive, innovative organization.

What matters here isn't the scale of the company—it's the internal shift. The same dynamic shows up in much smaller, more personal ways when you examine how you relate to talent around you.

From "Around Talent, I Can Feel Insecure" to "I Grow the Most Around Talented People"

This shift, from insecurity to growth, is central to embracing a Growth Mindset when surrounded by talented people who might otherwise intimidate you. It's also important to note that role models don't have to be perfect. They can have flaws and failures. In fact, not only can they have flaws and failures; ideally, you choose role models comfortable enough in their own skins that they share those flaws and failures with you. In doing so, they provide proof that our own flaws will not keep us from success, and they reinforce exactly which qualities we should admire and want to emulate. Having multiple role models in different areas of our lives provides a well-rounded perspective and inspiration to reach different goals.

My experience when I was partner at Startupbootcamp is a personal example of how a Fixed Mindset—feeling intimidated by others' success—can evolve into a Growth Mindset, where collaboration replaces comparison and inspiration thrives.

I had to reframe my own perspective on a colleague's success when I helped my partners Ruud Hendriks and Patrick de Zeeuw bring Startupbootcamp, a company that has now accelerated over 1,400 startups, to the United States in 2016.

Ruud and Patrick were both extremely successful before expanding to the US. They spent a big part of their careers at Endemol, one of the world's largest TV production firms. In 2010, they partnered to create Startupbootcamp, which grew into the largest accelerator in Europe, expanded to twenty cities worldwide, and a large portfolio of startups, amongst them unicorns. They then started two more companies together.

When they were ready to take Startupbootcamp to the US market, they went looking for a partner with entrepreneurial experience. I was that person. The three of us had an instant connection; we partnered in a newly created entity and started approaching US-based clients. But I quickly began to feel intimidated. Patrick had an unforgettable stage presence, with his long hair, Hawaiian shirts, and cowboy boots. Patrick and Ruud's stories were big and impressive, and Patrick's pitches blew people away. Each anecdote was more jaw-dropping than the last. When Patrick would travel back to Amsterdam, I was supposed to follow up with new leads. And I remember thinking: How do I possibly present after Patrick?

Using the success of others as an inspiration requires self-awareness and the ability to put your experiences and insights into perspective. I knew this intellectually, but it took some time to get there emotionally. In order to do so

I looked for my added value, which was around deeply understanding customer problems and seeing how those challenges could be addressed with our offerings. After Patrick had shared his inspiring work and established connections, the next phase was building relationships to enhance the sales process, and it was there that I could excel. We were, in fact, a perfectly complementary trio. After we found that balance, we built a lot of success together—success that would not have been possible if I had let myself be intimidated or discouraged by someone else's career, someone else's way of being their best self.

Whether it's working alongside industry leaders or tackling your own feelings of insecurity, the key is to reframe intimidation as inspiration. By doing so, you grow not just individually but collectively, creating opportunities for shared success.

From "They Won't Do a Good Job Unless I Tell Them How" to "Embrace and Value Where People Are"

This shift involves trusting team members to bring their unique skills and perspectives to the table, fostering creativity, and ownership.

Ed Catmull, co-founder of Pixar Animation Studios, exemplifies this shift. Early in his leadership journey, Catmull realized that micromanaging stifled his team's creativity. By insisting on control, he was limiting his team's potential and undermining the trust necessary for innovation.

Recognizing this, Catmull adopted a Growth Mindset, embracing the diverse strengths of his team members and creating an environment that valued open communication and collaboration.

One of Catmull's most impactful initiatives was the introduction of Braintrust meetings, where teams could present their projects and receive candid feedback. These meetings were grounded in the belief that great ideas could come from anyone, not just senior leadership.

By valuing his team's input and empowering them to take ownership of their work, Catmull fostered a culture of trust and creativity that led to groundbreaking films like *Toy Story* and *Finding Nemo*. His leadership demonstrated the power of trusting people to excel in their roles and underscored the importance of embracing individual contributions as a pathway to collective success.

Embracing Challenges Through Mindset Shifts

As the examples of Satya Nadella, and Ed Catmull illustrate, success is not just about achieving milestones; it's about the journey of growth, collaboration, and continuous learning along the way. Shifting mindsets is at the heart of this journey, whether it's moving from isolation to collaboration or from micromanagement to empowerment. These shifts require us to welcome vulnerability, trust our teams, and foster environments where creativity and innovation can thrive.

When you adopt a Growth Mindset, challenges become more than obstacles; they transform into opportunities to evolve both individually and collectively. By recognizing and addressing the Fixed Mindsets that hold you back, you open doors to stronger collaboration, and lasting impact. This is not only true for individuals but for entire organizations, where these shifts drive alignment, and growth at scale.

The shifts in this chapter aren't things you do once. They're things you practice until they stop feeling like shifts—and start feeling like how you lead.

In the chapters ahead, we will explore how to further identify and address the challenges that come with these mindset shifts, diving into practical tools and strategies that enable both individuals and teams. The path of growth is not easy, but it is always rewarding—and it starts with the courage to embrace the challenges that come your way.

Scan the QR codes below to access short RESET Leader videos that help you recognize growth barriers, shift mindsets, and experiment with new habits.

Growth Area: Success of Others

Learn how to turn comparison into inspiration and strengthen collaboration by valuing the strengths and success of others.

https://qr.resetleader.com/upFW6Q5i

Growth Area: Challenges

Discover how reframing challenges as opportunities helps you build resilience and grow under pressure.

https://qr.resetleader.com/WA0qppEK

CHAPTER FOUR

Set Up Habit-Shifting Experiments

The Power of Neuroplasticity: Effort Shapes the Brain

I've watched leaders agree on the need for change—and still walk back into the same meeting, with the same habits, and the same outcomes. Not because they don't care. But because insight doesn't automatically rewrite behavior.

Every meaningful change begins not with a grand gesture, but with a simple action. A shift in behavior. A small test. A new habit attempted. When we're serious about change—whether in how we lead, how we collaborate, or how we show up each day—it's not just about thinking differently. It's about doing differently.

That's what this chapter is about: the discipline and courage to *experiment*, and to set up habit-shifting actions that help us move from good intentions to real progress. These experiments don't have to be dramatic. In fact, the most powerful ones rarely are. They're small, intentional, and repeatable. And they offer the clearest path toward lasting change.

Show Up to The Gym (of Mindset)

Transitioning to a Learn-it-all approach isn't an instant transformation—it's a discipline. It requires effort, regular reflection, and the humility to start again when progress feels slow. Think of it like showing up to the gym. The membership itself changes nothing; it's just permission to begin. Real change happens when you show up, push through discomfort, and keep practicing when no one is watching.

Building a Growth Mindset works the same way. Reading about new mindsets is like signing up; applying them daily is the workout. Each time you choose curiosity over certainty, feedback over defensiveness, or experimentation over perfectionism, you're training the mental muscles that make change stick. Small reps—try, reflect, adjust—compound into resilience, and confidence.

Why start here? Because insight alone doesn't transform us. Action does. And more specifically, action that's structured like an experiment—where you test something new, observe its effect, and refine your approach—gives your brain the evidence it needs to believe *"This is working."*

"You Can Teach an Old Dog New Tricks": Beyond the Cliché

At first, this phrase may seem like a casual statement, but it holds a profound truth that science has now validated: We are never too old—or too set in our ways—to learn or change. This ability to change is possible because of neuroplasticity: the brain's capacity to rewire itself by forming new neural connections. Far from being "set in our ways," our brains are built to adapt. Every time we try a new behavior, we lay down a new path. Repeat that behavior, and the path gets stronger. Over time, it becomes a new default.

What I've seen again and again in practice—and what research later helped me put words to—is that effort changes the brain. Researchers like Dr. Michael Merzenich, known as the "father of neuroplasticity," have shown how deliberate mental effort—especially when paired with repetition—can literally reshape the brain at any age. Just as muscles strengthen through use, so do the neural circuits that support new thinking and behavior.

Imagine your brain as a living map. When you experiment with a new behavior—like giving more candid feedback or blocking time for reflection—it's like carving a fresh trail. At first, it's clumsy and slow. But with effort and consistency, that trail becomes well-worn, easier to access, and more automatic. This is why experimentation works: not because change is easy, but because the brain is built to reward what we reinforce.

One often-cited example is the study of London taxi drivers by Dr. Eleanor Maguire and her team at University College London. They found that years of navigating complex city streets physically enlarged the hippocampus, the part of the brain involved in spatial memory. The takeaway is simple: Effortful practice changes the brain.

But if this is true, if effort and experimentation lead to growth, why don't we all do it more often?

Because while the brain is willing, the mind often resists. And that resistance comes in the form of Fixed Mindsets that undermine our relationship with effort and risk.

What Gets in the Way of Experimenting?

This chapter explores how two specific growth areas hold us back—**effort** and **risk-taking**—and often sabotage our ability to set up and stick with habit-shifting experiments. The barriers to growth don't always show up as loud resistance. Often, they whisper: "Don't try too hard, you'll look weak." Or: "What if this doesn't work? Better not stick your neck out."

In the sections that follow, we'll unpack how these beliefs take root, how they hold back even the most capable professionals, and what mindset shifts are needed to move forward. Because without the willingness to invest effort—and take some risks—no experiment will stick. And without experiments, no transformation is possible.

What Gets in the Way of Effort?

As we all know, effort is the amount of energy and focus that we put into something. When striving to fully lean into a growth mindset, our relationship with effort is shaped by what we believe it says about us when we have to work harder than others to achieve similar results.

In her research, Professor Dweck discovered that high-achieving students and adults who'd been told that they were born geniuses, and who consequently believed that their skills and intelligence were native, and thus *fixed*, came to believe that these same inherent talents could not be refined or further developed. But once they found themselves, as we all do at one point or another in our lives, in a position where they actually had to put in substantial effort to learn something new, or had to take on a challenge that showed there was a limit to what they could do in that moment, their self belief was shattered. The result? They withdrew and fell back to the idea that they were unable to move forward because their natural talents could no longer carry them, that they had hit their limit. It seems to any objective observer like a contradiction, but this is how the psychology of Fixed Mindsets warps belief. Even though these high achievers were just as capable as anyone else—and arguably, even more so—of learning and mastering new skills, their own beliefs about themselves stopped them from doing so.

But this is not just academic. I've seen this play out in my own life. Like many parents, I often praised my children for being smart when they were younger. As a consequence, when they brought home good grades, they would proudly say it happened with little effort, because they believed their success was rooted in being naturally gifted. They began avoiding tasks they found challenging, fearing that struggle might reveal a lack of ability. Their focus shifted from learning and growing to protecting their image of being "smart," a mindset that inadvertently stifled their willingness to embrace new challenges and put in the effort required to master them.

Now of course, we know *intellectually* that this evolving growth is the normal way of things: we come up against challenges, we take the measure of what we need to learn, we learn it, and then we apply that learning to move forward. But Dweck is pointing out the plight of people who believed they could not develop their skills and intelligence further because they had been taught that their own ability to grow was not in their control.

These "born genius" children, who likely showed some early strengths that led others to say "You were born this perfect!" were then afraid to show that they were working hard. They became "fixed" in their belief that working hard must mean that they were *not* actually born geniuses, not as smart or talented as others believed them to be, and this led to shame: the counterintuitive shame that came from believing that they had some secret deficit and working hard was a sign of this. While we know, both objectively and *intellectually,* that this is merely normal human development, the psychological forces worked differently to turn what should have been an advantage into a trap.

While each of us may not have each been told that we were "born geniuses," many of us have been instilled with this Fixed Mindset to some extent and may have suffered as a result:

- "She's a natural athlete," even though it's the hours she has spent in practice that have brought out the skills seen on the field. When she faces a harder challenge with a new team, that label will "prove" to her that she's a fraud.
- "You're such a natural artist," which is only helpful until he tries to learn a new technique that takes some time to master; a "natural artist" would just be able to do it naturally, right?

These Fixed Mindset and beliefs about effort being a sign of inadequacy can then stay with us until we grow into adulthood. We will likely then take those beliefs subconsciously into our workplaces, especially if we are not aware of the toxicity of these beliefs.

A Fixed Mindset, often manifests in professional settings, where fear of judgment, perfectionism, and the stigma of "trying too hard" discourage leaders from putting in authentic effort. Most often these subconscious calculations about how we appear to others are centered on the risks to our own job and career. If we are hostage to these Fixed Mindsets, then we fear that if we put in effort—working harder, asking questions, showing less than 100 percent confidence in what comes next—people around us may notice us doing so.

We fear that being seen putting in effort might reveal our lack of experience or expertise—it may even make people think we are less intelligent, less worthy of the job we're in, and certainly not worthy of a promotion or a raise. That's a high cost. Our brains may decide that the benefit we might gain from asking questions or working harder, from a more collaborative approach or double-checking before acting, isn't worth the loss of face—even if doing so would be a significant boost to our understanding, or the larger goals of the company.

When we benefit from embracing a Growth Mindset, however, we come to understand that effort is required for mastery and success, and we evolve past the need to hide our so-called "inadequacies": We show no fear in inviting others into our learning journey. This is absolutely a necessary mindset shift to make if we want to thrive and succeed in business today. And any leader of any company or organization should want employees who are hungry to learn because that's where productivity and satisfaction comes from, and the leaders themselves should be just as—*if not more*—hungry to learn because they set the example for those below them.

Over and over across my career, I've seen how this can affect teams in even the most high performing companies. Quite often, this is particularly true of companies with competitive, lone wolf, genius-style cultures where the initial start-up was high profile and successful—followed by more and more of the work focused on building up a facade that hides fundamental vulnerabilities from the marketplace. This not only causes internal friction and stifles the possibility for teamwork, but it reinforces organizational silos across teams, departments, and business units, where the goal should be to break them down in order to foster long-term growth.

A real-world example of how a Fixed Mindset can stifle effort and hinder growth is the story of BlackBerry Limited. Once a dominant player in the smartphone market based on their first-in-class innovations of adding an actual keyboard and secure email to a cell phone, BlackBerry's early success led to a complacent belief in the superiority of their existing technology.

When Apple introduced the iPhone in 2007, it was a leap forward in concept and user experience: its touchscreen interface and app ecosystem were game-changers, but BlackBerry's leadership failed to recognize the need for significant adaptation and innovation. They clung to the notion that their existing tech was sufficient to maintain market dominance. This resistance to change and their inadequate effort to respond to new market demands caused BlackBerry to quickly lose its market share to more adaptable competitors.

- 2002: Blackberry launched its first phone with QWERTY keyboard.
- 2010: BlackBerry reached its peak in the US with 43 percent of the market and 41 million users globally (but Apple passed it in April 2011).
- 2014: BlackBerry's US market share dropped to below 3 percent.

By the time BlackBerry acknowledged the shifting landscape and attempted to pivot toward enterprise software and cybersecurity, it was too late to reclaim its leadership position in mobile devices. The company's story became a textbook example of how early success can breed overconfidence and how a Fixed Mindset can blind even the most innovative companies to the necessity of reinvention.

Today, BlackBerry survives in a different form, but its fate is a cautionary tale: In a world of constant disruption, effortful learning and continuous adaptation are not optional; they are the price of staying relevant.

BlackBerry's story isn't just a business case; it's a mirror. Many organizations, teams, and individuals face a similar tension: Do we stay the course, or do we risk effort on something new? Often, it's not a lack of resources or intelligence that holds us back; it's our mindset about what effort means. We hesitate to try something different, not because we don't care, but because we're afraid that the effort might not pay off, that all the energy we invest might somehow be wasted.

And that's exactly where the first mindset trap begins. BlackBerry wasn't alone. Blockbuster, another industry giant, fell into a similar trap. Once the country's largest movie rental service, they refused to see the changing landscape of video as services like Netflix began to crop up on the scene. Early success created a fear of wasted effort; a variation of the Sunk Cost Fallacy. Rather than adapting to changing demands, leaders doubled down on what had worked in the past—afraid, perhaps, that changing course would render their previous efforts meaningless.

This brings us to a common belief that holds many professionals back: Where do I put in effort, and where do I hold back?

"Effort" Mindset Shift #1

I Don't Want My Efforts to Go Down the Drain → There's No Such Thing as Wasted Effort

Let's take a closer look at the example of Blockbuster, whose downfall serves as a striking modern example of the Fixed Mindset "I don't want my efforts to go down the drain."

Despite the rising tide of digital streaming in the 2000s, business-darling Blockbuster, after almost two decades of market-capturing growth, clung to its traditional brick-and-mortar store for VHS/DVD-rentals model, fearing that embracing digital streaming would render its vast store network and past investments irrelevant. This reluctance to adapt led to its decline, overshadowed by forward-thinking younger competitors like Netflix, illustrating how a Fixed Mindset can hinder innovation and adaptation in a rapidly evolving industry—and lead to all past efforts going down the drain as well.

Notably, Blockbuster missed a pivotal opportunity when it was offered the opportunity to buy Netflix for a mere $50 million—a decision that suggests Blockbuster's leadership was so deeply immersed in justifying its own business model that it couldn't even entertain the idea that Netflix might also have a good growth idea and that Blockbuster would be the perfect foundation from which to launch the next-gen initiative. Blockbuster's growth, market experience, and already-built brand loyalty need not have been wasted, but Blockbuster needed to embrace the Growth Mindset to see this change as another step forward and up. *That's* the irony: the only way to protect past effort is to keep evolving.

The Blockbuster case reveals more than a missed business opportunity; it exposes how hard it can be to release what's familiar. For many of us, the fear that change might erase our past efforts quietly steers us away from growth. The fear of making a change that is part of rendering one's own existing skills and experiences irrelevant often prevents us from embracing new technologies or methodologies that are critical for staying relevant in today's fast-paced work environment. (And yes—every "born genius" company eventually gets its own test. Netflix will too.)

Shifting from a Fixed Mindset of fearing one's efforts will "go down the drain" and embracing the Growth Mindset that "There's no such thing as wasted effort" represents a profound shift in how we perceive our actions and their outcomes.

This shift in mindset underscores the recognition that every endeavor, regardless of its immediate success or failure, constitutes a valuable step forward on our individual paths of learning and personal development. It's not wasted effort; it's paid tuition. By successfully adopting this perspective, we learn to appreciate the intrinsic value in every effort, understanding that it contributes to the accumulation of experiences, insights, and resilience that propel us toward our goals.

This mindset encourages us to engage in our pursuits with confidence and openness, knowing that every action taken with integrity is an integral part of our continuous evolution and our journey towards mastery and self-discovery. Finally, perhaps most importantly for the RESET Leader, it instills in us empathy for our coworkers as they travel similar journeys under our leadership.

But for many professionals, showing that effort—especially when the work is unfinished or imperfect—feels risky. We hesitate to share early drafts, half-baked ideas, or works-in-progress not because we doubt their potential, but because we fear how they might reflect on us. This fear is rooted not in laziness, but in perfectionism: the belief that only polished, flawless outcomes are worthy of being seen.

Perfectionism doesn't just slow down iteration; it erodes confidence, silences creativity, and reinforces the mindset that effort should be hidden unless it produces something impressive. To build a culture where experimentation can thrive, we have to confront this barrier head-on.

Perfectionism and the Stigma of Showing Effort

At first glance, it may seem obvious that we should put in more effort before having other people look at a task, especially when it matters to us. Why would we not maximize our chances of success? Or at least get further down the road so that the potential is clear?

But research shows that as the perceived importance of a task rises, people are more likely to find themselves hesitant to put in effort due to their own sense of perfectionism. It's counterintuitive, but perfectionism has been linked to hiding effort at work—the work should just be perfect; we shouldn't have to try so hard—and perfectionism has been linked to increased depression and anxiety as well (Hewitt et al., 2017[4]; Curran & Hill, 2019[5]).

It has also been linked to higher levels of job burnout, workaholism, and decreased work engagement (Stoeber & Damian, 2015[6]). All of this research makes it clear enough that perfectionism and a Fixed Mindset about showing your effort can be damaging toward a company's culture, teamwork, employee engagement, employee mental health, and overall business performance.

---

[4] Hewitt, P. L., Flett, G. L., & Mikail, S. F., *Perfectionism: A Relational Approach to Conceptualization, Assessment, and Treatment* (New York: Guilford Press, 2017).

[5] Curran, T., & Hill, A. P. (2019). Perfectionism is increasing over time: A meta-analysis of birth cohort differences from 1989 to 2016. *Psychological Bulletin*, 145(4), 410–429.

[6] Stoeber, J., & Damian, L. E. (2015). Perfectionism in employees: Work engagement, workaholism, and burnout. *Personality and Individual Differences*, 82, 41–46.

Distinguishing Between Harmful Perfectionism and High Standards for Work

While one might think that perfectionism keeps the quality and standard of work high, researchers have discovered that there are two main factors to perfectionism, one that has a positive impact and one that has a negative. Perfectionistic Striving is a positive attribute—it's a desire to make the work as *good as it can be* within the framework of getting it done. Perfectionistic Concerns, however, are more problematic—that's where we may believe that we are lacking and become fixated on our mistakes, or are unable to finish our work out of a belief that there is some *perfect* aspirational end product that we, mere humans that we are, will never achieve. Perfectionistic Concern is essentially another mindset that holds us back.

Studies confirm that those who lean toward those negative Perfectionistic Concerns had lower levels of work engagement and higher levels of job burnout, while those who lean toward the positive Perfectionistic Strivings—the setting of perhaps higher-than-necessary standards and goals but still understanding that getting something out in the world is paramount—actually had *higher* levels of job engagement and *lower* levels of burnout.

So yes: Keep setting high goals and standards for your business and your teams!

And yet, be mindful as well: If you want your organization to truly perform collaboratively and without silos, while you set those high standards, you must also check to see if you detect that Fixed Mindset of Perfectionist Concern. If you do it, you can RESET: recognize it, shift away, and stop fixating on the negative idea that working harder means you are not good enough, then embrace the Growth Mindset that learning and growth are a continuous process of self-improvement.

Leaning into that mindset is not always easy. When I was the CEO at GOS International, an engineering firm I had co-founded, I struggled with my own expectation that I should have all the answers for my team and my colleagues. What I brought to the table was a set of skills that fit my position: business development and sales. Whenever we had to make decisions regarding product improvement or innovation, I had to rely on the expertise of my colleagues with engineering backgrounds.

In hindsight, I can see that that is perfectly fine. That's why we had those colleagues on our team; our skill sets were complementary! At the time, however, I felt like I should be the one to deeply understand all of the technical aspects of our products—despite my lack of technical engineering expertise—but the truth was, my knowledge only went so far. This made me feel insecure, like I was just the "business guy" who couldn't contribute much to the technical side of things. In meetings, I often stayed quiet rather than taking the risk of asking what might be perceived as dumb questions.

This know-it-all mindset came back to bite me when we engineered a 16-color industrial offset printer for a major client. The pressure to get the machine to market was intense, and we shipped it without fully addressing all of the engineering mistakes we had made during development. The machine initially appeared successful, but it failed to reach the expected production output.

My business partner, who was also the head of engineering, was absent due to burnout, leaving me to navigate meetings with the client's plant people on my own. I was too afraid to admit my lack of expertise and expose what I worried would seem like a "rookie approach" toward the project, so I made the decision to focus solely on the commercial side of things and to just assume that the engineering specifics were all perfect.

This decision had far-reaching consequences that I didn't fully comprehend at the time. The machine's failure meant that we had to come to an agreement for compensation because we delivered a machine that didn't entirely live up to the original agreement, and we cut ourselves off from the opportunity to continue developing and tapping into a growing market. In the end, my inability to embrace my lack of expertise and ask important questions, my decision to rely solely on a fear-based overconfidence led to missed opportunities and the potential for irreparable damage to our business's reputation.

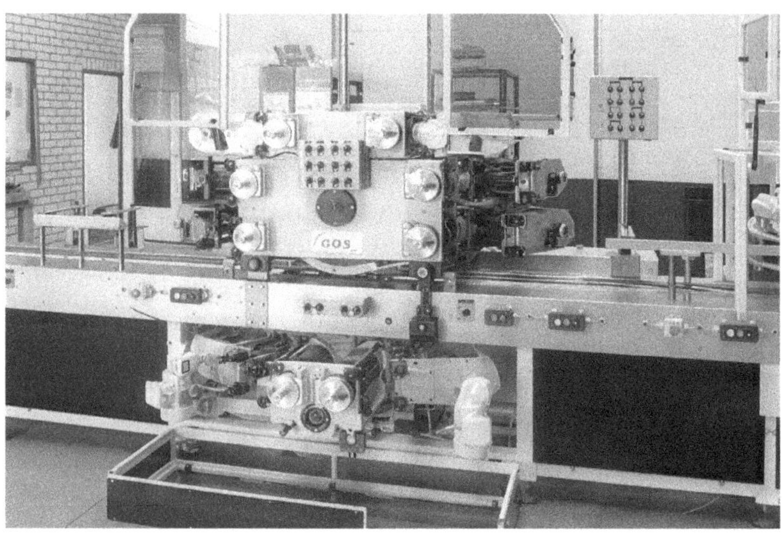

(The Machine: 16-color High Speed Industrial Printer for Egg Boxes. I'm still not entirely sure how it works.)

"Effort" Mindset Shift #2:

Geniuses are Born, Not Made → Hard Work Beats Talent Any Day

The story of Kodak's decline offers a stark example of the Fixed Mindset, "Geniuses are born, not made." As pioneers in the photographic film industry, Kodak initially developed the first digital camera in 1975 but hesitated to embrace the digital technology they had created. Their leadership believed strongly in their historical institutional genius in film, underestimating the necessity of continual innovation and adaptation to maintain market leadership in a rapidly evolving industry.

This scenario mirrors Blockbuster's—and a common pitfall for many individual professionals: resting on early successes without continuing to evolve their skills or adapt to new environments. Many professionals may feel that once they have achieved a certain level of expertise or recognition, further effort is unnecessary. However, just as Kodak missed the shift toward digital photography, individuals can miss emerging trends and technologies that could impact their careers if they are not doing the hard work of keeping up with the evolving landscape.

Transitioning from the Fixed Mindset belief that "Geniuses are born, not made" to the Growth Mindset conviction that "Hard work beats talent any day" represents a fundamental shift in how we perceive success and adaptability. This mindset encourages the understanding that ongoing effort, persistent learning, and adaptation are critical, even for those initially seen as "geniuses" in their fields.

Encouraging "Effort" in Your Organization

Putting in authentic effort requires willing to face risks (of looking less competent) and to tackle challenges (of completing the difficult task). This is especially true in an unsafe company culture that sees effort as a sign of a lack of intelligence or skill. If a company wants to encourage employees to put in effort—and therefore maximize their individual and collective chances of success—that company needs to create a culture that prioritizes learning above knowing.

There are plenty of benefits that come with building an environment safe for people to embrace putting in effort, and those benefits accrue to both the company and the individual. There are many examples of people putting in effort somewhere lower in the organization's hierarchy that led to breakthrough innovations that benefited the business as a whole tremendously.

For your individual professional success, effort is essential. When you put in effort and work hard, you are more likely to produce high-quality work, build trust, credibility, and collaborative relationships with colleagues and clients, access greater opportunities, and improve your overall job performance and satisfaction. All of that is possible ... as long as you are in an environment where learning and effort are valued.

Vulnerability

The journey from shifting mindsets around effort is pivotal for both organizational success and for personal growth.

I imagine you are gleaning that organizational success is less likely—and often not long-lasting—without the personal growth. And the key to personal growth—and to embracing effort, in particular—is *vulnerability.*

By being vulnerable, knowing we are imperfect, and doing the best we can because the imperfection is actually integral to what we bring to the table, by recognizing and confronting our ingrained perceptions that equate effort with inadequacy, we unlock the potential for continuous improvement and achieve greater resilience. And that makes the organizational successes possible.

The stories of companies like Kodak and Blockbuster remind us that our greatest barriers often stem from a reluctance to venture beyond comfortable norms and embrace the rigorous demands of innovation and learning.

I am not, of course, disregarding bottom lines or end results. All of these efforts are aimed at specific goals, even when the goal is simply to explore.

Vulnerability is what makes effort visible, but it's also what prepares us for the next step: risk-taking. When we set up habit-shifting experiments, effort gets us moving, but it's *risk* that truly tests whether we're willing to grow. Every meaningful experiment carries some risk—of failing, of being judged, or of having to change course. But without risk, effort remains confined to the safe and familiar.

To move forward, we have to be willing to stretch beyond what's comfortable. Risktaking isn't a separate act from experimenting; it's built into the very structure of trying something new.

From Experimentation to Risktaking: A Natural Progression

Experimentation, as we've explored, is the process of setting up small, manageable actions to test new behaviors, gather evidence, and refine our approach. It's a low-risk, high-value strategy that builds momentum through small wins. But experimentation doesn't happen in a vacuum—it requires us to step outside our comfort zones and confront the uncertainty of trying something new. This is where the concept of risk-taking becomes critical.

Risktaking is the backbone of experimentation. Every experiment, no matter how small, involves a degree of risk: the risk of failure, the risk of wasted effort, and the risk of exposing vulnerabilities.

Yet, as the science of neuroplasticity reminds us, our brains need this feedback to grow. Without taking risks, we remain stuck in familiar patterns, unable to build the neural connections or the behavioral habits that drive real change. Risktaking is not about gambling or reckless decisions: it's about embracing calculated, informed risks as a path to growth.

From Gambling to Growth

It's important to understand that not all risks are created equal. Some risks propel us forward; others set us back. I learned this lesson the hard way.

In 2004 at a trade show in Asia, I came across a technology that caught my eye. Seiko Epson had developed an inkjet printing technology that could be applied on an industrial scale, removing many of the disadvantages of conventional printing. My partners and I saw the opportunity to develop applications for this printing technology in a wide spectrum of industries, so in 2005 we set up Tinct, a startup to commercialize these newly developed applications.

Our initial market research had shown us that an application for the promotional products industry could be promising. Within six months we had our first Industrial Digital Printer ready, the Tinct Sprinter, a machine the size of a twenty-foot shipping container. You could feed the machine with a tray of promotional products like key chains, magnets, or pens, and they came out completely digitally printed on the other side within seconds. We were sure that the Tinct Sprinter was going to revolutionize the $20 billion promotional products printing business.

It was a complete flop. We made the classic mistake of starting with a solution and then having to find our way to a client; our chances of hitting the mark were slim-to-none. After a few years, as with thousands of others of great ideas that have flopped, Tinct went defunct.

We had not been risktaking; we had been *business gambling.* We didn't perform our due diligence with customer research; we didn't take reasonable risks by cutting development into small incremental steps to validate with potential customers.

Why Risktaking Matters in Behavioral Change

Embracing reasonable risk is not just a strategy for organizational innovation, it's essential for personal and behavioral transformation. When it comes to experimenting with new habits, thought patterns, or ways of showing up at work, risk-taking shows up in subtle but powerful ways. Every time you test a new behavior—whether it's speaking up in a meeting, giving feedback more directly, or changing how you lead—you're taking a risk. A risk of being misunderstood, of failing, or of standing out.

The good news is, these kinds of risks don't require us to overhaul everything at once. When approached intentionally, behavior change can begin with small-scale experiments. These micro-tests allow us to observe what works in low-stakes environments and refine our approach without overcommitting or disrupting everything around us. The goal is to learn by doing, without gambling our credibility or confidence.

A structured process like the Build–Measure–Learn loop, often used in innovation but equally effective for personal growth, can help break down complex changes into manageable, testable actions. Instead of waiting for perfect conditions or total clarity, this approach encourages people to act, reflect on outcomes, and iterate. It's especially useful in large organizations where entrenched habits and institutional inertia make even small changes feel risky. But when risk is framed as experimentation, not exposure, resistance softens.

This mindset isn't just for leaders guiding strategy. It applies to anyone trying to unlearn an old habit or adopt a new one. You don't need to stake your reputation or your role—you just need to start with something small and be willing to learn from the result. That's what healthy risk-taking in behavioral change looks like: intentional, reflective, and grounded in curiosity, not fear.

But while this principle is easy to admire in hindsight, it's much harder to embody in real time—especially when the change we're considering is personal.

Because you're closer to the consequences than large companies, taking risks feels harder—making your mindset even more important. For individuals and teams, risk-taking often means challenging behaviors that have felt safe or successful in the past. It means being willing to leave behind familiar ways of working and confront the discomfort of the unknown. And when that discomfort kicks in, it's often our underlying mindsets that determine whether we move forward—or retreat. Let's look at the most common mindsets that hold people back from taking meaningful risks in how they think, behave, and lead.

"Playing It Safe" Isn't Safe

The ability to hit that RESET button—to start again because what we've learned in this iteration makes it clear that a RESET will lead to better outcomes—is precisely a comfort with taking risks. We cannot *know* that we will be more successful; we can only know that we have weighed the risk and found it reasonable.

Put another way: If you are reading this book, there is likely something about your business or the work you do that you would like to improve. Improvement means change. Change literally means doing something that we haven't done before, and that will always require some level of risk: that our plans will not unfold as we anticipate, or that unforeseen challenges may emerge. But change is a process that has inherent momentum. It is the path to something new. If you believe in "playing it safe," then you won't be able to adapt to change or innovate; you will be stuck and you won't improve.

And we don't want to be changing all the time. Or even most of the time. Most of the time, we are looking for consistency and predictability in our business operations—the more predictable our operations, the lower the risk, and the bigger the chance we won't burn up or miss the mark. While we all know that taking risks is part of creating a unique value proposition and an offering that differentiates us from our competitors, still, most of us will instinctively avoid Risktaking; it is unpredictable and messy. It could cause the business to implode.

So we naturally tend to be more risk-averse than risk-loving, especially when our business has seen some success and has become sizable enough for us to care about losing what we've gained. And that's when risk aversion starts to thrive. We need to actively combat this aversion if we want to keep moving forward at speed, stay atop the wave, and lead our field of expertise. Otherwise there is a good chance we'll end up like some of the notable companies that failed to take risks—that played it safe by assuming their particular view of the marketplace couldn't be wrong:

- **Sears:** They failed to adapt and innovate in the face of the rise of digital marketplaces, the rise of discount stores like Walmart, and the growth of smaller independent brands. Once the world's largest retailer, Sears has just crawled out of bankruptcy and is in the process of liquidating its once great assets.
- **Tower Records:** Once a great chain store selling music in 200 retail locations worldwide, Tower Records management played it safe by sticking to their brick-and-mortar strategy despite the rise of digital music sales ... and there hasn't been a Tower Records anywhere since the last physical US location closed in 2006.
- **BlackBerry:** At its peak, BlackBerry owned almost half of the US smartphone market. But they played it safe by keeping to their original smartphone design with a physical keyboard, and when the full-sized touch screen took over the market, BlackBerry's decision doomed the company. They have been officially out of the smartphone business since 2017.

In each of those cases, the marketplace shifted beneath the company. The company, in response, thinking it was more prudent to continue with business as usual, did not react in time. So how do you become comfortable taking risks so that you not only survive the inevitable changes in the marketplace, but can use the momentum of change to achieve your ambitious growth goals? One antidote is to change your mindset from "Play It Safe" to "No Risk, No Reward."

"Risk" Mindset Shifts #1:

Play It Safe → No Risk, No Reward

Shifting from a Fixed Mindset of "Play It Safe" to a Growth Mindset of "No Risk, No Reward" is fundamentally about altering how we view risk and opportunity. This shift is not about recklessness but about moving from seeing stasis as "safe" and, instead, leaning into the potential that lies within calculated risks. It involves a conscious decision to evaluate opportunities through a lens of potential growth and learning, rather than through the fear and avoidance that companies such as Sears and BlackBerry chose.

This mindset acknowledges that while not all risks will lead to success, the journey toward significant achievements often begins with the willingness to step out of one's comfort zone. It champions the idea that strategic risk taking is essential for progress, encouraging us to weigh the benefits and drawbacks of potential actions thoughtfully—and then to place our bet on the future.

Practice: Small Bets

One effective strategy for reinforcing the best kind of Growth Mindset risk-taking is called "*small bets.*" It's about breaking down ambitious goals into manageable, bite-sized experiments: tests that let us learn quickly without committing full resources. This approach reduces risk, accelerates learning, and keeps teams focused on progress rather than perfection.

By adopting the small bets strategy, you foster a learning mindset within your team, model that mindset for the broader organization, and keep the customer—or purpose—at the center of every decision.

We often associate breakthrough success with bold, all-or-nothing moves. But some of the world's most transformative companies grew through the quiet discipline of small bets.

Take Google, for example. Larry Page and Sergey Brin didn't set out to build a trillion-dollar enterprise. Their big dream—organizing the world's information—began as a small research project at Stanford. Their first prototype, BackRub, was a crude algorithm that simply analyzed how web pages linked to one another. It wasn't beautiful, and it certainly wasn't finished. But it worked—just a little better than what existed before.

That one small bet gave them evidence worth pursuing. They built a basic search engine around it—still imperfect, still clunky—and tested it with real users. Over time, each new feature, from Gmail to Maps to Android, followed the same rhythm: prototype, test, learn, and iterate. None of these innovations were guaranteed successes. They were all small bets: informed experiments that grew into monumental change through continuous learning.

That same principle applies in leadership. When leaders encourage small bets, they create psychological safety for experimentation. People stop waiting for permission and start testing ideas. They stop aiming for flawless plans and start learning through feedback.

I've seen this in organizations we have worked with—from startups to multinationals—where the teams that grow fastest are those that learn fastest. They don't fear failure because they've reframed it as information. Every experiment, whether it succeeds or fails, adds to their collective intelligence.

The lesson is simple but powerful: Transformation doesn't come from betting everything on one big move. It comes from many **small, intentional acts of learning**—repeated, refined, and scaled.

"Risk" Mindset Shift #2:

Why Stick My Neck Out? Nothing Good Comes From It → Challenge the Status Quo

Status quo is Latin for "existing state." Like all states of being, it has two sides. Optimistically, the stability of the status quo can offer safety and, assuming there's some kind of a growth curve to that status quo, a continuing beneficial condition; pessimistically, the status quo can be a place of safety that people fear to question. That "existing state" of a particular workplace's culture can be hard to define, especially for the people who are deep within, "fixed" (if you will) within it. Because of their Fixed Mindset, the norm feels universal—almost eternal. In those situations, we will hear people say, "That's just how things are done around here."

Of course, we know that just because something has been done a certain way for a long time doesn't mean that it's the best way, or even a good way, of doing things. This thinking can trap an organization into doing things ineffectively, and it discourages people from sticking their neck out because it can carry a sense that veering from the status quo—even questioning what has, thus far, brought good returns—is to endanger what little safety the market can offer. In fact, the more turbulent the market, the more people are often hesitant to hit that RESET button—no one wants to go from the safety they can feel into something that holds no hope of safety. If it's in the stormy seas that we discover our boat isn't seaworthy, then we need to be prepared to take to the seas in *some* other way.

Transforming how you think—from a Fixed Mindset of wondering "Why stick my neck out?" to a Growth Mindset that seeks to "Challenge the status quo"—represents a pivotal shift from a similar stance of risk aversion and complacency toward one of active engagement. This transition is about moving beyond the comfort of the known and the conventional in order to question, disrupt, and reimagine what is considered standard or given. It underscores the importance of not just accepting things as they are in hopes of avoiding disruption but, instead, being driven by the curiosity to explore how they can be improved or transformed.

Embracing this mindset is about recognizing that true growth and groundbreaking advancements often require stepping into uncharted territories, challenging existing norms, and being open to the possibilities that such challenges may unveil. It encourages a culture where proactive change is valued, and individuals are empowered to seek out opportunities for improvement, leading to a dynamic environment where growth and breakthroughs are not just possible but actively pursued. And it all starts with deciding to make a break.

When we explore and question a workplace's culture—which includes processes and systems—we ideally dive into its history and can determine if it is still relevant in our current state and, more importantly, if it is relevant to reaching our desired state. By digging deeper, we may uncover truths about those systems or the goals we've set; owning these truths may lead us to another path and open up whole new worlds we never imagined before. Growth happens by staying open to all kinds of possibilities—ideas that we may not even imagine are possible realities given the current state of a project or organization. If we're leaping from the boat, then, we need to be able to calculate the possibility that there's a way to land.

If a low-risk culture is deeply embedded, change can feel difficult and dangerous. Challenging with intention, rather than fear—for example: "I'd like to see what the team can come up with that's outside the box"—is more likely to elicit a positive response from those who are still hesitant, or at least an openness to explore other viewpoints and ideas. Constructively challenging the status quo is an opportunity to begin conversations and explore new ideas, opening the door to transforming the way programs and services are delivered, how business is done, and how the culture of an organization shapes its performance.

Let's choose one major workplace structure—the team meeting—as an example. Team meetings are where much of workplace culture is set and reinforced; leaders lead and, in doing so, they model what is important to the organization. If that leadership is toward unquestioning allegiance to the status quo, the message is heard loud and clear. If that leadership is toward shared imagining and challenging with intention, then the message is quite different.

Practice: Psychological Safety

One way to challenge the status quo and foster an environment of psychological safety—a space where people can speak up and share ideas without fear—is to rethink how we run our team meetings.

Meetings shape the emotional tone of an organization: how we listen, how we react, and how we value each other's input.

In our work with leadership teams, one pattern kept showing up–teams that learned fastest weren't the ones avoiding mistakes, but the ones surfacing them early. I found language for this pattern in the research of Amy C. Edmondson,[7, 8] a professor of leadership and management at Harvard Business School, whose work on psychological safety helped explain what we were seeing in practice. Her research showed something surprising: The highest-performing teams actually reported more errors than the lower-performing ones.

At first, it seemed counterintuitive: Why would better teams make more mistakes? But when she looked deeper—and we saw this play out with teams ourselves—it became clear that teams weren't failing more; they were *speaking up* more. They felt safe enough to report errors, admit uncertainty, and ask for help without fear of blame. That openness

[7] Edmondson, A. C. (1999). Psychological safety and learning behavior in work teams. *Administrative Science Quarterly*, 44(2), 350–383.

[8] Edmondson, A. C. (2018). The Fearless Organization: Creating Psychological Safety in the Workplace for Learning, Innovation, and Growth. Hoboken, NJ: John Wiley & Sons.

created faster learning, higher trust, and ultimately, better outcomes.

The insight reshaped how we understand team effectiveness. High performance isn't about eliminating mistakes—it's about creating an environment where mistakes can surface quickly, be discussed honestly, and become learning opportunities.

In leadership, that means creating the same kind of safety zone in our own teams. Whether through regular reflection moments, "no-blame" reviews, or open debriefs, we can model what Edmondson's teams practiced every day: curiosity over certainty, learning over image, and transparency over silence.

Meetings are one of the most powerful places to start. They're where RESET Leaders bring people along in the process—announcing new initiatives, testing small bets, and reflecting together on what's working and what's not. When psychological safety is present, meetings shift from being moments of performance to moments of transformation.

In those moments, you can feel the shift: People lean in, not away. Ideas get sharper, not safer. And growth becomes a shared act of courage.

Scan the QR codes below to access short RESET Leader videos that help you recognize growth barriers, shift mindsets, and experiment with new habits.

Growth Area: Effort

Understand how valuing effort over talent changes how you learn, collaborate, and make meaningful progress.

https://qr.resetleader.com/gER6tIdF

Growth Area: Risk Taking

Learn how to work beyond your comfort zone, take informed risks, and experiment safely in uncertain situations.

https://qr.resetleader.com/YHWQmGe5

CHAPTER FIVE

Examine New Behavior Impact

The Role of Results

I've seen people do the hard part—change their behavior—and still walk away unsure whether it mattered. That uncertainty is no accident. When you step outside your comfort zone, discomfort is inevitable. It whispers doubts: *Am I capable? Will this work? Should I retreat*? Yet, growth isn't about immediate comfort—it's about what happens when you persist. The proof of success, however small, transforms discomfort into confidence. Without examining the impact of your efforts, these moments of proof can go unnoticed, leaving discomfort unresolved.

Albert Bandura, a renowned psychologist, offers a powerful explanation for this phenomenon in his theory of self-efficacy. According to Bandura, our belief in our ability to succeed in specific situations—our self-efficacy—is shaped largely by mastery experiences. These are tangible moments of success that provide direct evidence that we're capable. In plain terms: Confidence grows when we see ourselves make progress. Every time we complete a task, overcome a challenge, or try something new and see progress, our confidence grows.

The Power of Small Wins

Bandura offers a useful lens for understanding this: Experiencing small wins directly impacts our confidence. These "proofs" validate our efforts and show that stepping into discomfort can lead to success. On the other hand, failure to reflect on or notice these small wins can erode confidence. Without that moment of recognition, discomfort remains unresolved and may even discourage further attempts.

I remember vividly the first time I facilitated a Growth Mindset workshop with a team of executives. I had spent weeks preparing: drafting materials, rehearsing delivery, and imagining how to handle questions. But as I walked into the room, I felt a familiar tension in my chest. *What if they don't find this valuable? What if I lose their attention?* The discomfort was real, and for a moment, I questioned whether I was ready.

What kept me moving forward was a focus on delivering value, even if imperfectly. I took a deep breath, started the session, and embraced the vulnerability of sharing new ideas. Midway through, something surprising happened: an executive interrupted—not to challenge me, but to share how much the framework I had introduced resonated with a current challenge they were facing. Their response sparked a rich discussion, and by the end of the session, participants were openly sharing how the workshop had shifted their thinking.

That moment—a participant's validation of the framework—was my proof. It showed me that stepping into discomfort had been worth it. That single interaction transformed my uncertainty into confidence and reinforced my belief that I could guide leaders through complex discussions. It was my first experience of mastery as a facilitator, and it fueled my desire to refine my methods and expand my impact to even more leaders, which I can see now was the first step in the journey of building Growthstars.

Looking back, the real shift didn't come from preparation alone. It came from examining the impact. From noticing what landed. From allowing evidence—however small—to replace doubt.

Why Mastery Experiences Matter

Bandura's research demonstrates that successfully completing tasks outside one's comfort zone reinforces self-belief. These experiences don't need to be dramatic breakthroughs; even the smallest success can motivate further effort and persistence. This creates a positive cycle: Small wins fuel confidence, which drives us to take on bigger challenges, leading to more wins and greater growth. Over time, this cycle compounds. What once felt uncomfortable becomes familiar. What once felt risky becomes part of how you lead.

Looking back at that early workshop, I realize the impact of that moment wasn't just the success itself, but the clarity it provided. By examining the impact of my efforts—listening to the feedback and seeing the results—I let the evidence register. That's when trust shifted: Not just trust in others, but trust in *myself* to lead transformative conversations.

As you reflect on your own growth, consider this: What are your mastery experiences? What small wins have validated your efforts and proven that stepping into discomfort was worth it? By recognizing these moments, you can transform hesitation into confidence, one success at a time.

Without that reflection, discomfort stays unresolved. And unresolved discomfort has a habit of pulling us back to old behaviors.

Step 4 of RESET is about finding those sparks of proof. By intentionally examining the impact of your experiments, you turn effort into evidence. And evidence is what allows confidence to grow.

Why Examining the Impact Matters

Experiments are only as valuable as the insights they generate. Without taking the time to reflect and validate outcomes, you risk missing opportunities for growth. Examining the impact answers critical questions:

- Did the new behavior create the desired change?
- How did it affect relationships, team dynamics, or performance?

- What adjustments should be made for greater effectiveness?

It's also about building emotional resilience. Seeing positive outcomes—even small ones—reinforces your commitment to new behaviors. Without this reflection, discomfort can feel pointless, and the experiment risks being abandoned.

Feedback plays a pivotal role in recognizing these mastery experiences. Often, the "proof" we seek comes from others' perspectives—whether it's a colleague expressing appreciation, a team member improving their performance, or a simple acknowledgment of progress. These external validations are like mile markers on the road of growth, reminding us that we're moving in the right direction.

The Mirror of Growth

Feedback is your first and most reliable tool for examining impact. It provides the external perspective we might not see on our own and serves as a mirror, reflecting our progress or blind spots.

However, feedback is often misunderstood. Feedback is more than just open communication or directness, as some cultures might perceive it. It goes beyond simply having an open door policy where individuals feel free to express any thought or criticism at any time. At its most basic, feedback is information given to you about your performance or behavior that helps you to adjust and improve. It can be positive, negative, or neutral.

Feedback comes from supervisors, peers, or even through self-assessment and reflection; it can be delivered verbally, non-verbally, or in writing. In psychological theory, feedback plays an important role in learning and developing skills and abilities. In everyday leadership, we often underestimate this and operate on assumption.

True feedback involves a structured and thoughtful approach to giving and receiving information that is constructive, specific, and aimed at growth and improvement. It requires empathy and consideration for the recipient's feelings and context, ensuring that the feedback is not only well-intentioned but also delivered in a manner that can be effectively understood and acted upon. Simply speaking one's mind without regard for the impact or without offering actionable insights does not constitute genuine feedback—it's discharge and feels like noise, not learning.

Therefore, while openness and direct communication are important aspects of a feedback culture, they must be accompanied by a deeper understanding of how to deliver feedback effectively to achieve meaningful outcomes.

Fear of Feedback

The foundation of this shift is realizing that feedback is not criticism. Feedback and criticism are related but distinct concepts, since feedback is information given about a person's performance or behavior that aims to help them improve and make adjustments. Criticism, on the other hand, is an evaluation of a person's performance or behavior that is usually focused on identifying flaws or shortcomings.

But criticism can be negative or constructive. The main difference between feedback and criticism is the focus and tone. Feedback is focused on helping someone improve, while criticism identifies areas to improve but does not aim to help the person do so. Feedback is usually delivered in a more neutral or supportive tone, while criticism may be delivered in a negative or confrontational tone. Yet in practice, the distinction often collapses.

Understandably, people often dislike and avoid criticism for several reasons: fear of rejection, as it can trigger feelings of being unwanted or excluded; threat to self-esteem, as it may feel like a personal attack on one's identity; emotional reactions, including anger, embarrassment, and frustration, which can complicate processing and response; perception of fairness, with criticism often seen as unjust if not constructive; and lack of context, making it challenging to interpret and leaving room for confusion and frustration.

Because these two concepts are related, people confuse them. And since criticism can be unpleasant and is often not constructive, people may find it difficult to receive feedback when they see it as criticism.

Giving feedback, especially in a professional setting, poses several challenges. Fear of confrontation can lead to hesitancy in delivering potentially critical feedback, undermining the opportunity for constructive dialogue. Moreover, varying communication styles among team members can contribute to misunderstandings during feedback exchanges. Power dynamics within organizations can influence the effectiveness of feedback, with authority figures exerting more influence over the feedback process.

Finally, inadequate training on feedback practices within many organizations deepens these challenges, resulting in less effective feedback loops.

Since both giving and receiving feedback can be fraught, many leaders shy away from it. Not because they don't believe in it—but because the emotional cost feels too high. In contrast, when feedback is embraced and understood in the context of a Growth Mindset, it can add enormous value to an organization.

Feedforward

Feedback that is only focused on past performance can actually do more harm than good. Research shows that when people receive feedback on poor past performance—what they *should* have done—they actually end up with a lower motivation to change, and it also damages the relationship between the feedback giver and recipient (Gnepp et al., 2020[9]). Put simply: Looking backward often drains energy instead of creating it. Thus, feedback that focuses on future performance, which actually motivates and inspires, is the only way that we train our clients and their organizations to embrace the power of feedback.

Having established the foundation of feedback within an organization, it's important to explore how industry leaders implement this crucial element to foster growth

[9]Gnepp, J., Klayman, J., Williamson, I. O., & Barlas, S. (2020). The future of feedback: Motivating performance improvement through future-focused feedback. *PLoS ONE*, 15(6): e0234444. https://doi.org/10.1371/journal.pone.0234444.

and innovation. One of the most inspiring case studies on cultivating a feedback-rich culture comes from Netflix. In his book *No Rules Rules: Netflix and the Culture of Reinvention*, co-founder and former CEO Reed Hastings outlines how the company built a culture centered on radical candor and continuous feedback. The book, co-authored with Erin Meyer, explores how Netflix challenges conventional management practices by embracing transparency, freedom, and accountability at scale.

At Netflix, feedback is not merely encouraged—it's expected. Hastings advocates for "radical candor," a principle that combines direct, honest critique with genuine care for colleagues' growth. This approach is practiced through regular 360-degree feedback sessions where employees receive input from peers, supervisors, and subordinates alike. The outcome is a multi-dimensional understanding of performance that strengthens both individual development and team collaboration.

What's important here is not the mechanism, but the signal it sends: Feedback is normal and ongoing. It's part of the work and not a judgement on the person.

Another unique practice is the *Keeper Test*, where employees are encouraged to ask their managers: "If I were to leave, would you fight to keep me?" If the answer is no, the ensuing conversation provides clear, unfiltered feedback—offering the employee a choice: improve or move on. This tool reflects Netflix's commitment to high performance and cultural alignment, ensuring that those who stay are either already thriving or deeply committed to growing.

When Feedback Becomes Culture

What makes Netflix's example relevant to RESET Leader is how clearly it demonstrates the impact of mindset on behavior. By normalizing candid, multidirectional feedback and anchoring it in trust, Netflix cultivates a culture where growth isn't incidental—it's systemic. Leaders who adopt Growth Mindset principles can learn from this: Radical transparency and continuous evaluation are not just operational tactics, they are mindset shifts that unlock high-performance environments.

Feedforward works because it keeps dignity intact. It shifts the conversation from "what went wrong" to "what do we try next?"

As we reflect on the Netflix' case, one truth becomes clear—feedback isn't just a tool, it's a *mindset*. It's not something you schedule once a year; it's how learning shows up day to day.

To foster this kind of environment, RESET Leaders must challenge and reframe the fixed beliefs that often undermine feedback. In our work, we frequently encounter three particularly persistent Fixed Mindsets that limit this—and three corresponding shifts that unlock it.

The first is the belief that *talking about problems will just slow us down*. Many teams hesitate to surface issues, fearing it will derail momentum or provoke discomfort. The result is false calm—everything looks fine, but deeper issues remain. Small issues are left unresolved, accumulating silently until they grow into crises. This avoidance doesn't save time; it costs it, compounding friction and draining energy.

The shift comes when leaders embrace the mindset: *We can't improve if we don't talk openly and quickly about problems.* Seen through this lens, raising issues is no longer a sign of negativity or resistance—it's a necessary act of ownership. Silence doesn't protect momentum; It quietly erodes it. When problems are addressed early, the team can align quickly, adjust course, and maintain speed without sacrificing trust. This shift fosters transparency, trust, and a proactive rhythm of continuous improvement—hallmarks of a high-performing, feedback-driven culture.

The second mindset barrier sounds like this: *"Getting feedback"* is code for *"I've failed."* For many, the act of receiving feedback triggers shame or self-doubt, as though it reveals a fundamental inadequacy. This perception encourages perfectionism and discourages collaboration. People wait to share their work until it's "flawless"—a costly delay in fast-paced, innovative environments. And worse, that delay often disguises stagnation.

The growth-oriented shift reframes feedback entirely: *Share work before it's ready.* By doing so, we unlock the power of iteration. Early feedback invites perspective and sharpens thinking. It turns exposure into acceleration. It's not a signal of failure, but a sign of maturity. A leader who is secure enough to improve in plain sight. This shift builds a culture where feedback is normal, welcome, and even energizing. It encourages co-creation, speeds up learning cycles, and dismantles the illusion that excellence happens in isolation.

This brings us to a third, closely related mindset: *It's not ready until it's perfect.* Even seasoned executives who know the value of feedback can struggle with this one. The idea that something must be polished to perfection before it's shared is rooted in fear—fear of judgment, fear of losing credibility, fear of being exposed as less than flawless. Perfection becomes a shield.

This drive for perfection often leads to delays, stress, and missed opportunities. Work gets refined endlessly, while valuable input is deferred. Ironically, it's this very pursuit of perfection that undermines quality and agility.

Shifting to a mindset of *progress over perfection* is subtle but changes everything. It affirms that what matters most is forward momentum—learning through action, not waiting for certainty. Progress means sharing drafts, experimenting openly, and allowing feedback to guide development. Perfection asks, "Is this safe to show?" Progress asks, "What can I learn next?"

This shift accelerates development cycles and lowers the psychological cost of feedback. It creates a work environment where people take smart risks, iterate quickly, and build resilience through constant learning. Most importantly, it aligns perfectly with the RESET approach—where iterative habit-shifting and reflection lead to deeper transformation. Perfection freezes learning; progress keeps it alive.

These three shifts point in the same direction: making it safe to be honest about what's not working. That sounds simple. In most organizations, it's the hardest thing there is. And they remind us that feedback isn't a flaw-revealing mechanism—it's a growth-revealing one.

Throughout my professional career, I struggled with feedback as well. I wanted to appear smart and competent to partners, employees, clients, and even people in my personal life. I confused being intelligent with having the answers. It wasn't until I changed my beliefs around intelligence that I started to be comfortable reframing what being intelligent meant—focusing on *learning* instead of *knowing*. It helped me to change how I perceive feedback, and now I actively seek insights and corrections to improve my work, performance, and even relationships.

Throughout my work with organizations, I've seen many enterprises put a high value on feedback, often training the workforce in it as a regular practice, since embracing feedback works best when it's embedded in the culture. What that requires is to be very clear about what feedback really means and what the most effective context for feedback is so it can be practiced in an ongoing way, year round.

To create that constructive company culture that supports feedback, you first need to create psychological safety. People experience psychological safety when they know they won't be penalized or shamed for sharing ideas, asking questions, or making mistakes. It's not something you announce—it's something leaders model, repeatedly. Leadership needs to continuously improve psychological safety to create an environment where people feel comfortable speaking up and sharing feedback without fear of judgment or retribution. When employees feel safe and supported, they are more likely to embrace feedback as a means of learning and growing, rather than as a threat to their self-esteem.

More than anything else, appreciating feedback is critically important for growth. And it's also one of the most challenging aspects of the RESET Leader because it requires a high level of self-awareness and the courage to stay open when it feels uncomfortable.

Where Are You in the Game?

As we discussed in Chapter 4, when we explored the role of *Effort* in setting up habit-shifting experiments, a powerful insight comes from *The Trillion Dollar Coach* by Eric Schmidt, Jonathan Rosenberg, and Alan Eagle. Through the book, Bill Campbell—a trusted advisor and executive coach to many of Silicon Valley's top leaders—returns us to a deceptively simple coaching lens: "Where are you in the game?" Are you watching from the audience, executing as a player, or stepping back to coach the game?"

In the context of *Effort,* this question helped us reflect on how the roles we take on—whether observing, supporting, or executing—shape our learning and growth. But when viewed through the lens of *Feedback,* the same question takes on a new dimension: It becomes a prompt for understanding how we influence the growth of others.

If you're in the audience, you're watching. You may be invested emotionally, but you're removed from the flow of feedback and decision-making. Still, even from the stands, your presence and energy can shape the tone and momentum of the game.

If you're a player, your focus is singular: execution. You're in motion, absorbed in performance, often too close to the action to see the full picture or offer meaningful feedback to others.

But as a coach on the sidelines, your role shifts. You see the whole field. You create strategy, observe patterns, and offer targeted feedback to elevate each player's contribution. You're close enough to influence outcomes but far enough to remain objective and supportive.

Effective leadership means learning to shift roles intentionally. To foster a feedback-rich culture, we must spend more time coaching than doing, *guiding* rather than *directing*. That means stepping back to make space, offering timely and constructive feedback, and resisting the urge to have all the answers.

So ask yourself: *Where am I in the game right now?* And where do I need to be to help my team develop?

By becoming more conscious of the roles we play, we can help shape cultures that value feedback, and nurture continuous learning.

Fear of Failure

Feedback inevitably brings up what didn't work, and this is where most of us struggle. We equate failure with incompetence, but in reality, failure is data. It's feedback in its rawest form.

When I visited the pop-up Museum of Failure in Brooklyn, New York, I was struck by the profound insights it offered on the role of failure in the journey toward success. The museum, founded by Dr. Samuel West, a Swedish psychologist and researcher in innovation and organizational behavior, aims to destigmatize failure and inspire us to take meaningful risks. One display highlighted the fact that all progress requires an acceptance of failure, while marveling that, because of our human vulnerabilities, the fear of failure can be paralyzing to the point of stalling that very progress.

The museum reminds us that innovations fail for many reasons, whether it's because of corporate hubris, poor leadership, bad design, or simply bad luck. Each failure, however, carries a valuable lesson. Educator and author Stephen Covey wrote, "If there's one thing that's certain in business, it's uncertainty." That has always resonated deeply with me; Covey's insight emphasizes the fundamental and unavoidably unpredictable and intertwined nature of success and failure.

Speaking in terms of the internal challenges we encounter in striving to make our dreams real, a powerful perspective from Brazilian novelist Paulo Coelho reminds us that "There is only one thing that makes a dream impossible to achieve: the fear of failure."

The experience of immersing myself in the Museum of Failure underscored for me the crucial importance of not just recognizing but *embracing* failure as a necessary step toward growth and innovation. Also crucial is the dream, the innovation, the change that we are striving toward; the point is not to fail for the sake of failing, hoping that something good comes of it, but rather to dream big, set our sights on what we might achieve, and include failure as an absolutely certain part of the equation, the business plan, the understanding-behind-the-scenes for making it all happen. This work, the success and failures, the effort and the setbacks, the feedback and the resilience—*it's all about the endgame.*

Let's explore the vital role of failure in fostering resilience, driving growth, and—here's the endgame!—achieving extraordinary outcomes, drawing on both historical examples and modern-day ventures.

As I wandered through the exhibit's "celebrating" failure, I couldn't help but think of high-profile figures like Donald Trump. Long before his presidency, Trump's business ventures saw a series of failed products and companies—Trump: *The Game*, Trump University, Trump Steaks, Trump Resorts, and Trump Shuttle among them. Most of these efforts tried to cash in on his persona more than offering real innovation, and many ended in lawsuits or market rejection. The takeaway isn't simply that Trump failed often, but that these failures reveal little about learning or transformation. Whether in business or politics, his pattern raises a deeper question: Are we pursuing something meaningful enough to endure failure, or just betting on visibility?

Elon Musk offers a different lens. Famously declaring, *"Failure is an option here. If things are not failing, you're not innovating enough,"* Musk has built companies like PayPal, Tesla, and SpaceX on a foundation of risk, setback, and iteration. His journey includes being ousted from Zip2 and PayPal, repeated rocket crashes, and very public stumbles—yet his capacity to treat failure as fuel is part of what drives real breakthroughs. One of his latest ventures, X (formerly Twitter), may turn out to be a flawed grudge match or a misunderstood experiment in free speech—but unlike Trump, Musk is still very much in motion. In five years, what looks like failure today could prove foundational to something else entirely.

These examples underscore that while failure is inevitable, it's not inherently redemptive. What matters is the *why* behind our efforts. As leaders, we must choose goals worthy of failing for—missions that stretch us, teach us, and elevate our work. When failure becomes a teacher instead of a verdict, it moves us toward resilience, clarity, and ultimately, more meaningful success.

What Failure Actually Is

Failures are, like more intense versions of risks we take or challenges we encounter, annoying, unnerving, uncontrollable, and headache-inducing. Sometimes we can guess where we'll encounter them, and sometimes they seem to come out of nowhere—things are going well, and then suddenly the universe throws a metaphorical banana peel in our path. Sometimes we can even experience multiple banana peels at the same time.

Where a *challenge* (as we explored in Chapter 3) is a formidable task or daunting set of circumstances, a *failure* is when our attempt to tackle the challenge not only didn't work well, it made things worse, brought things to a standstill, trashed the plan we'd worked out and the calendar we'd depended on.

For the moment, let's set aside the discussion of the fact that it is likely only a momentary failure—in that moment, a failure is, well, a failure; it has all of the weight of loss and grief, and it is a place from which it is difficult to have perspective. And yet—similar to stepping into vulnerability and healthy *risk-taking* (as we explored in Chapter 4)—if we use the Mindset Shifts as tools, they can get us through the moment of failure and into the reframing of the setback as merely a point along the arc of our lives.

The Importance of Reflecting on Failures

In the business context, failures are not just unavoidable; they are essential for growth. What matters is not the failure itself, but whether we slow down enough to learn from it. Failures provide critical insights into what went wrong and why. They reveal flaws in strategies, processes, and assumptions, offering a clear roadmap for improvement. By analyzing failures, businesses can identify gaps in their knowledge and skills, paving the way for targeted learning and development.

Many groundbreaking innovations are the result of lessons learned from failures. When something doesn't work, it pushes us to think creatively and explore alternative solutions. Real progress rarely comes from getting it right the first time—it comes from repeated attempts that sharpen our understanding. Our creativity needs iterative cycles—spaces to try, learn, and keep going until we find something new that works. Reflecting on failures fosters a culture of experimentation and risk-taking, essential for staying competitive.

Facing and overcoming failures by continuing until we find success builds resilience. It teaches individuals and teams to handle adversity, and persist in the face of challenges. Resilience is a critical trait for long-term success, enabling businesses to weather storms and emerge stronger.

Success alone can sometimes lead to complacency, where past achievements create a false sense of security—this is an echo of the "born a genius" problem we discussed back in Chapter 4. Reflecting on failures keeps businesses grounded and alert to potential pitfalls—and reminds us all that the goal is learning and growth toward a better understanding of whatever we're working on.

It's only a slight tangent to point out that even countries such as the United States are built on the idea of striving toward "a more perfect union"—part of the genius of this founding document is its notion that perfection is never finished. That same principle applies to organizations and leadership. Whether we're looking at our business or our statecraft, continuous reflection and improvement prevent stagnation and promote growth.

The Difficulty of Reflecting on Failures

And yet: reflecting on failures is inherently challenging for several reasons. Firstly, failures often come with a heavy emotional burden. Our own feelings of disappointment, frustration, and even shame can cloud our ability to objectively analyze what went wrong. Admitting failure can be a blow to our ego and self-esteem, making it difficult to confront and accept mistakes. And since there is a natural human tendency to avoid negative experiences and focus on positive ones, this bias can lead us to downplay or ignore failures instead of facing them head-on, setting up cycles of shame rather than iterative cycles of solutions.

All of this intensifies if the team or company leader lets us know our failure is unacceptable. In a professional setting, there can be fear of repercussions, such as losing credibility, respect, or even one's job, which can discourage open discussions about failures.

The societal and organizational culture plays a key role in all of this. Many workplaces prioritize success and perfection, often punishing failure rather than treating it as a learning opportunity. This creates an overall environment where individuals feel compelled to hide or minimize their mistakes rather than reflect on and learn from them. What suffers first is learning; what follows is stagnation. That inability to reflect and improve is unhealthy for the individual—and can be *disastrous* for the organization.

Reflecting on failures is inherently challenging, but it's also essential for growth. By adopting a Growth Mindset, we can begin to see failures not as endpoints, but as stepping stones; critical moments that offer insight, redirection, and potential. This shift in thinking allows us to respond to setbacks with curiosity instead of fear. To support this transformation, let's explore several mindset shifts that can help us reframe failure.

In many organizations, the prevailing belief is that "Failure isn't tolerated." This Fixed Mindset stems from a fear of mistakes and their potential repercussions—loss of reputation, diminished credibility, or even job termination.

The emphasis is on avoiding errors at all costs, which leads to a culture where individuals become reluctant to take risks or pursue new ideas. Even when there are good structures for feedback, as we explored earlier in this chapter, the fear of failure can quietly undercut experimentation. People hold back—not because they lack ability, but because they've learned that failure is unsafe. What gets lost is the energy that comes from trying something new, not knowing how it will turn out, and learning in the process. Innovation quietly dies under the pressure to "Get it right."

When we shift this mindset to "Our failures are celebrated as learning opportunities," we embrace the idea that failures are not endpoints, but doorways. This Growth Mindset understands that every failure offers valuable insights. It encourages us to reflect, share, and adjust. By celebrating—not in the sense of glorifying failure itself, but recognizing the courage and learning behind it—we create a culture where it's safe to try. And when it's safe to try, it becomes easier to reflect. People speak more openly, learn more quickly, and take bolder steps. The organization becomes more adaptive, creative, and ultimately, more successful. In this kind of environment, we don't fear failure—we use it. We extract value from it. And we move forward with more insight than we had before.

Another deeply embedded belief is that we have to "Get it right the first time." It sounds responsible, even noble. But in reality, this mindset can be paralyzing. It leads people to spend excessive time planning, overthinking, and polishing ideas that never make it into the world. They delay action because of the pressure to be flawless, and that pressure crushes experimentation. When we believe that every move has to be perfect on the first try, we avoid making any move at all.

This is why the shift to "Don't worry about failure—you only have to be right once" is so important. It frees us to take action, to experiment, and to let go of perfectionism. Most meaningful progress doesn't come from getting it right immediately. It comes from trial and error, from testing and adjusting. When we internalize this mindset, we stop trying to predict the perfect answer, and we start creating better ones by moving forward. It accelerates our learning, invites input, and makes room for serendipity. The project doesn't have to be perfect. The process just has to stay in motion. And once something works—once that breakthrough happens—it doesn't matter how many attempts it took to get there. What matters is that we stayed in the game long enough for it to happen.

The final mindset we'll explore here is the sense that "When we crash, we burn." It's the idea that failure is catastrophic—that one mistake could unravel everything we've built. This mindset is rooted in fear: the fear that failure is final, and the fear that we won't recover. It sees failure as something that must be avoided at all costs, not because of the pain itself, but because of what we think it says about us. If we fail, maybe we're not good enough. Maybe we're not meant to lead, or build, or grow. And when this belief takes hold, it keeps us from taking any bold steps at all.

But when we shift toward the mindset that "We get right back in the ring," we begin to see failure differently. We see it as something we can recover from—and often, something we must recover from. It's not the end of the story. It's a plot twist. Getting back in the ring means refusing to let one failure define the journey. It means accepting that failure is part of progress, and that the real test of leadership isn't how we avoid it, but how we respond when it happens. This shift builds resilience. It builds teams that don't flinch at the first sign of trouble. And when this mindset is part of a culture, it changes everything. People feel braver. They take risks. They try again. And they learn that failure isn't something to fear—it's something to learn from, together.

Failure in Practice: Ray Dalio, Bridgewater, and "Radical Transparency"

The benefits of embracing our decisions, learning from our mistakes, and questioning our assumptions is nowhere more clear in the example of Bridgewater Associates, one of the world's largest hedge funds. Under the leadership of Ray Dalio, Bridgewater has built a culture centered around the concept of "radical transparency" and continuous learning.

Dalio's principle of "radical transparency," and an institutional emphasis on what he calls "believability-weighted decision-making," have allowed Bridgewater to thrive by embedding learning into every part of the decision-making process.

The Bridgewater Approach

Dalio's approach, as detailed in his book *Principles*,[10] involves systematically recording the decisions made within the company, along with the rationale behind those decisions. This structured documentation has created a feedback loop, helping employees and leaders alike reflect on past decisions to inform future ones. In effect, decisions are never final—they remain open to examination. This creates a log that can be analyzed to understand decision-making patterns, biases, and outcomes over time.

Implementing the Learning Culture

At Bridgewater, every meeting and significant decision is recorded. This radical openness gives employees the freedom to challenge ideas and share their insights. Employees are encouraged to critically evaluate each other's decisions and thought processes, effectively creating a real-time feedback system of predictions, outcomes, and reasoning. This level of transparency can feel uncomfortable, especially in environments where being wrong has historically carried a cost, but it ultimately strengthens decision-making. This database serves

[10] Dalio, Ray. (2017). *Principles: Life & Work*. New York: Simon & Schuster.

as a learning tool, enabling employees to refine their decision-making skills by understanding where their predictions went right or wrong.

The Results of Radical Transparency

This culture of transparency and accountability has been a key factor in Bridgewater's success. Employees are less afraid to make bold predictions or decisions, knowing that the emphasis is on learning and improvement rather than punishment for being wrong. Psychological safety here is not about comfort—it's about permission to learn in public. This fosters innovation and pushes the organization toward continuous evolution. The firm's ability to innovate and adapt to changing market conditions has been significantly enhanced by this approach. By focusing on learning from both successes and failures, Bridgewater has built resilience into its decision-making processes.

From Discomfort to Resilience: The Failure Resume

In the professional world, we often focus on our successes, highlighting achievements and accomplishments on our resumes. However, creating a "failure resume" can be a powerful exercise in self-awareness and growth. A failure resume lists the significant failures and setbacks you've encountered, along with the lessons learned from each experience.

Acknowledging failures fosters humility, which is often the missing ingredient in real learning, making us more open to feedback and growth. It helps build a culture where mistakes are not hidden but shared for collective learning. Reflecting on past failures helps identify recurring patterns and underlying issues that need addressing. It provides a clear picture of areas where improvement is needed, guiding personal and professional development.

Understanding past failures equips us with better problem-solving skills for future challenges. It encourages a proactive approach to identifying and mitigating risks. When leaders are willing to name their own failures, they give others permission to do the same. Sharing your failure resume can inspire others to embrace their own failures and learn from them. It builds a supportive environment where everyone feels empowered to take risks and innovate.

Growth isn't achieved by avoiding discomfort or failure—it thrives because of them. When we examine the impact of our actions, we find the evidence we need to reinforce our confidence, recalibrate our efforts, and trust the process. Feedback serves as our mirror, revealing our progress and offering insights we can't always see on our own. Failure, in turn, provides raw, unfiltered data about where adjustments are needed.

The failure resume is one of the most practical ways to put this mindset into action. By documenting your setbacks and extracting the lessons within them, you build self-awareness and model the kind of leadership that makes learning visible. Failures aren't endpoints—they're stepping stones.

Imagine a workplace where leaders openly share their failure resumes. Such transparency cultivates psychological safety, fosters trust, and normalizes learning from mistakes. It sets a powerful example: When leaders embrace their own fallibility, they inspire others to take risks. This culture of collective learning doesn't just tolerate failure—it uses it as a launchpad for progress.

Step 4 of RESET challenges us to go beyond mere action. It asks us to pause, reflect, and validate—turning discomfort into confidence and setbacks into breakthroughs. By recognizing the impact of your efforts, welcoming feedback, and embracing failure, you not only grow as a leader but also create an environment where everyone feels empowered to experiment, adapt, and thrive.

As we conclude this chapter, it's worth remembering that the journey through feedback and failure are not detours from performance. They are the mechanism through which performance improves. Together, they lay the groundwork for lasting transformation.

The next chapter is about the final step of RESET, where we shift from experimentation to integration and focus on transforming successful habits into sustainable working rituals. This step is about embedding what works into daily practice, so progress becomes repeatable, and durable over time.

Scan the QR codes to access short RESET Leader videos that help you recognize growth barriers, shift mindsets, and experiment with new habits.

Growth Area: Feedback

See how inviting feedback early and often accelerates learning, improvement, and trust.

https://qr.resetleader.com/4V8iPDr9

Growth Area: Failure

Learn how to respond to setbacks with curiosity, extract learning from failure, and build resilience over time.

https://qr.resetleader.com/1KMld6Rr

CHAPTER SIX

Transform Successful Habits into New Working Rituals

I've seen teams run powerful experiments—change real behaviors—and still watch the impact fade six months later. Not because the work didn't matter. But because nothing held it in place.

As we reach the final step of the RESET process, the focus shifts from short-term experimentation to long-term sustainability. This is where growth becomes embedded, not just as a momentary success, but as an enduring part of how we lead, and collaborate.

Transforming successful habits into new working rituals is about embedding a culture of continuous learning—and doing so intentionally. It's not enough for change to happen in the moment; it must be captured, codified, and repeated. That's what Step 5 of the RESET process delivers: a transition from loose experimentation to structured reinforcement. Habits live with individuals. Rituals live with teams. When we repeat the right behaviors often enough, they become rituals. And rituals are how culture is scaled.

In our work with leaders, their teams, and organizations, I've seen how rituals become shared systems that make strategic alignment automatic. Teams stop relying on motivation or memory. Instead, the work itself reminds them how to behave. Practices like test-before-perfect, feedback-in-the-moment, or weekly user-value delivery become default behaviors—because they're built into how work happens.

When we do this well, participants consistently report a shared sense of alignment, autonomy in decision-making, access to the information they need, and clarity in their roles. They also feel that everyone's voice is heard equally and that their work is delivering tangible value—such as shipping value to users weekly.

These aren't just positive experiences. They're *signals.* They tell us the system is working; that learning, ownership, and execution are no longer dependent on individual heroics. They're the markers of a culture built for continuous growth and sustained success.

The practices we adopt and embed must become part of the fabric of how we work, lead, and collaborate, fostering a culture of continuous learning. Habits rely on intention. Rituals remove the need for it. A habit asks, "Will I remember to do this?". A ritual answers, "This is simply how we work here." Because the real test isn't whether a behaviour works once—but whether it survives the moments when it's inconvenient.

Persistence is the fuel that turns habits into rituals and growth into permanence. It's what leaders model when they keep showing up—especially after the novelty wears off. It's the quality that keeps us moving forward, even when initial excitement fades or when challenges threaten to derail progress. Without persistence, even the most well-designed experiments and strategies risk becoming fleeting moments of success rather than long-term transformations. Persistence does not mean stubbornly repeating what no longer works. It means staying committed to the outcome while remaining flexible about the path. This step invites us to embrace persistence as a core principle. It is our last and eight area to develop the Growth Mindset.

From Habit to Ritual: What Actually Changes

A habit becomes a ritual when it no longer depends on personal discipline. It's no longer something individuals remember to do; it's something the system *expects*. This is where many change efforts quietly stall.

Teams run pilots. Leaders model new behaviors. Results improve. And then—slowly, almost imperceptibly—old patterns return. Not because people don't believe in the change, but because the organization never made space for it to live on. Rituals solve this by removing choice at the wrong moment. They don't rely on motivation, alignment meetings, or reminders. They show up in calendars, agendas, decision rules, and ways of working. They make the desired behavior the default, not the exception. In other words, rituals shift the burden of change from people to structure. And that's what allows progress to survive pressure.

In this chapter, we will explore how persistence, driven by a Growth Mindset, becomes the bridge between fleeting improvement and enduring change. Not by doing more—but by staying with what matters long enough for it to take root.

From Habit to Ritual → From Personal Growth to Culture Shift

Rituals are the memory of your organization. They make excellence repeatable and strategy executable—at speed.

I've learned that persistence isn't about heroic effort. It's the ability to stay with something long enough for it to matter—especially when progress slows, resistance shows up, or certainty disappears. What separates strong leaders isn't intensity, but endurance. It's not just their intelligence or charisma, but their willingness to stay engaged when momentum fades. They remain committed and engaged over time, even when the path gets difficult.

Psychologist Angela Duckworth calls this quality "grit". In her book *Grit: The Power of Passion and Perseverance,*[11] she highlights this as central to achievement. Her work shows that those who succeed at high levels—whether in demanding training programs or high-stakes competitions—tend to sustain both effort and interest over the long haul. What unites them is not just discipline, but direction.

In my experience, leaders who persist are often anchored by a clear vision—a purpose that acts as a compass in turbulent moments. They also demonstrate strong self-awareness; they know their limitations and are willing to seek support when needed, whether by drawing on internal team strengths or bringing in outside expertise. Persistence shows up as *collaboration,* not *stubbornness.* They value collaboration and foster a culture where shared learning and mutual support are part of how progress happens.

In today's fast-moving business environment, this kind of persistent leadership is vital. It's not about grinding blindly forward. It's about staying committed to a meaningful goal, adapting intelligently along the way, and bringing others with you through a combination of resilience and humility.

It's a Marathon, Not a Sprint

In the spring of 2010, I received a call from an executive at Fuji Seal International, a company known for its labeling

[11] Duckworth, Angela. (2016). *Grit: The Power of Passion and Perseverance.* New York: Scribner.

and packaging systems. They were planning a bold collaboration with Chobani—a relatively new yogurt company that was already disrupting the U.S. market.

At the time, most yogurt cups were decorated using low-cost dry-offset printing. But Chobani's founder, Hamdi Ulukaya, had a different vision. He wanted cups that stood out on the shelf—fully labeled, premium packaging that would signal the brand's quality. It was a more expensive and complicated route, and most suppliers were hesitant. Fuji, however, was all in. They quickly developed two pilot labeling lines but needed external equipment to handle and transport cups efficiently between labeling, inspection, and packaging stages.

That's when Fuji called us. At GOS International, we had the technical experience they needed to design this kind of cup-handling system. The deadline was tight. We had to use a mix of new and used machines, improvise, and scale fast. Despite our doubts about meeting Ulukaya's aggressive targets, we took on the challenge.

Once production began, things got harder. At low speeds, the system worked. But at full speed, tiny variations in airflow caused endless interruptions. Our team worked around the clock—adjusting airflows, reprogramming sensors, video-recording cup movements down to the millisecond. Every fix introduced a new variable. Every hour brought new problems.

And yet, we kept going. Every failed cup, every production halt became another data point. We stayed with it, not because we had a perfect solution, but because we believed one would emerge. And eventually, it did: 25,000 labeled cups per hour, 5 million per week, two lines running smoothly. Chobani was able to execute its scale-up, and we were proud to have played a part in making it happen.

This project drove home what I've come to believe deeply: Success is a *marathon*, not a *sprint*. Persistence wasn't just about leadership vision—it lived in how the team kept adjusting, learning, and showing up, again and again. And that's the lesson here: Persistence is not a solo trait reserved for founders or CEOs. It's a cultural trait. It's what propels organizations forward through complexity, uncertainty, and fatigue.

Persistence as a Growth Mindset in Action

Persistence is a concrete manifestation of the Growth Mindset. When we adopt a Growth Mindset, we believe that our skills and abilities can be developed through effort and experience. This mindset helps us persevere because we view every step of the journey, no matter how monotonous or challenging, as a learning opportunity that prepares us for what comes next. Rather than perceiving setbacks as insurmountable, we see them as invitations to grow.

This belief—that effort leads to learning and learning leads to growth—fuels behaviors and attitudes that are synonymous with persistence. And yet, within organizations, persistence often breaks down not because people lack ambition, but because subtle Fixed Mindsets get in the way. These mindsets—quiet, familiar, and often normalized—can erode commitment before effort even begins. Let's explore how some of these internal narratives shape the way people engage with difficult work and how subtle mindset shifts can turn hesitation into momentum.

The Short-Term Trap: When "Quick Wins" Kill Persistence

"Focus on quick successes" or "Pick the low-hanging fruit" is a mindset that has permeated many organizations, especially in a world increasingly focused on short-term results. At first glance, this approach seems useful; it allows teams to see immediate results and can serve as a motivator to move forward. Indeed, this bias toward immediacy crowds out the deeper work that actually produces lasting value.

However, when short-term results become the dominant operating mode, it erodes persistence. Teams become hesitant to take on deeper challenges that stretch timelines and comfort zones. The long game is abandoned in favor of visible wins. And perhaps most importantly, this mindset leaves little room for learning from failure—because the priority is speed, not reflection. In a "quick win" culture, mistakes are inefficiencies to be avoided rather than wisdom to be mined.

A Growth Mindset invites a different orientation: "It's a marathon, not a sprint." This is more than just a platitude—it's a philosophy of pacing, endurance, and investment in things that matter. A marathoner knows the race isn't won in the early miles. It's won through consistency, through resilience when fatigue hits, through planning for the inevitable dips. Likewise, leaders and teams with this mindset understand that progress worth making is often invisible at first. It builds slowly and reveals itself in hindsight.

This orientation allows people to value gradual learning, small wins, and strategic patience. It encourages celebrating steady progress, not just final outcomes. And more importantly, it creates space for persistence to emerge naturally—not forced through pressure, but invited through a commitment to something that's bigger than a moment.

While quick wins might give a temporary dopamine hit, the marathon mindset cultivates stamina. It creates cultures where people stay engaged even when results aren't immediate, because they believe the work has meaning and momentum beyond the short term. In this way, persistence becomes part of the culture's emotional rhythm—embedded, expected, and respected.

I Procrastinate ... And That's a Problem

But sometimes persistence doesn't break down because of speed or scale—it breaks down quietly. One of the most common and often overlooked corrosive signs of a Fixed Mindset in organizations is procrastination. It's often dismissed as a time management issue, but underneath it lies something deeper.

Within organizations, an awakening sense of being locked into a Fixed Mindset often surfaces in the form of this concern: "I procrastinate, and that's a problem." The broader Fixed Mindset—where employees believe their abilities are static and limited—can drive this behavior. When failure is perceived as a verdict on one's worth, delay becomes a shield. By postponing action, individuals avoid the risk of exposure or critique. In environments where mistakes are punished or perfection is the norm, procrastination becomes a self-protective strategy.

Over time, this erodes persistence. When tasks feel too risky, ambiguous, or high-stakes, they get pushed aside—not because people don't care, but because they're trying to survive emotionally. Reactivity replaces initiative. Delays become default. Innovation slows down not because of laziness, but because of fear.

A Growth Mindset rewires this impulse. The mindset that *I am responsible for my work from start to finish* reclaims agency. It shifts the narrative from fear to ownership. This isn't about perfectionism or micromanagement—it's about a deep commitment to the full arc of contribution. It means: *I begin even when unsure. I adapt when things break. I keep going, even when it's hard. I own not just the wins, but the setbacks too.*

In the context of persistence, this mindset is transformative. It doesn't just ask someone to start; it invites them to stay—through uncertainty, feedback, and the moments when progress and doubt creep in. It recognizes that challenges are part of the process, not proof of inadequacy. Every obstacle becomes an invitation to refine, to continue. This sense of responsibility sparks proactive behavior—not because the work is easy, but because it matters.

Ownership cultivates resilience. Instead of waiting for ideal conditions, individuals with this mindset step forward. They make progress in imperfect settings, take initiative amidst ambiguity, and continue even when motivation wanes. This isn't the loud persistence of heroics—it's the quiet, daily kind that moves organizations forward.

The contrast between "I struggle with procrastination" and "I am responsible for my work from start to finish" is stark. One leads to avoidance and stagnation. The other builds momentum and meaning. When teams internalize this shift, the impact is cultural. A sense of collective ownership emerges. People stop waiting to be told and start choosing to contribute. Tasks become missions. Accountability becomes shared.

This shift opens the door to a resilient, responsive culture, one where employees don't just finish what they start—they become stewards of the entire journey. They take pride in their process and trust their ability to adapt. They feel empowered to move forward—especially when the path is unclear.

Making Habits Stick: From Practice to Ritual

Not every habit becomes a ritual. In our work with leadership teams, we've found that good intentions fade unless the system carries them. For a behavior to truly embed into culture, five conditions tend to be present. Use this as a checklist when you're ready to turn an experiment into an enduring practice:

It's not dependent on one person
The ritual still happens even if the original initiator is absent.

It happens on a rhythm
There's a defined cadence—weekly, bi-weekly, monthly—that makes the behavior feel inevitable.

It's visible
The team sees the behavior in action or experiences its results consistently.

It's connected to purpose
People understand why it exists—it serves something bigger than just process.

It helps us grow
The ritual drives learning, not just repetition. It feeds back into how we evolve.

I Must Not Be Cut Out for This

Ownership creates the platform. It places responsibility in the hands of the individual and the team. But once ownership is embraced, the next challenge often becomes stamina. The question becomes: Will we stick with it, especially when it gets difficult?

That's where another form of Fixed Mindset often appears, quietly and convincingly: "Pushing through is too tough." This is the voice that whispers when energy wanes and outcomes stall. The road feels longer than expected. It tells us the problem isn't the challenge—it's us. That we don't have what it takes. That perhaps we've overreached. It's not just doubt; it's resignation.

This mindset is especially dangerous because it sounds reasonable. After all, pushing through is hard. But when we equate difficulty with futility, we rob ourselves of the resilience we've likely already demonstrated in other areas of our life. And in doing so, we miss the chance to stretch, and grow.

In a Fixed Mindset, the obstacle becomes proof of inadequacy. Instead of saying "This is hard," we unconsciously start saying "I must not be cut out for this." This is where persistence breaks down—not because of the size of the mountain, but because of the belief that we don't belong on the climb.

By contrast, a Growth Mindset sees difficulty as part of the contract. The belief that "It takes determination and dedication to get to the top of the mountain" reframes the struggle not as a sign of failure, but as the necessary terrain of progress. Persistence, in this frame, is not optional. It's expected—because it is a part of who we are *becoming.*

This belief doesn't deny hardship; it dignifies it by making effort meaningful, not a judgment about us. It reminds us that everything meaningful is built through sustained effort. The airplane, the microchip, the moon landing—all once impossibilities until someone chose to keep climbing.

It's not about heroic endurance. It's about repeated, focused commitment over time.

When individuals internalize this mindset, they begin to welcome challenges. Not because it's easy, but because they understand the link between difficulty and transformation. They don't interpret obstacles as personal failure. They see them as part of the recipe.

This is what persistence looks like in practice. It's not glamorous. It's not loud. But it is powerful. It shows up every time someone finishes a hard project, navigates a tough quarter, or leads a team through complexity without giving up.

The shift from "Pushing through is too hard" to "It takes determination and dedication" is foundational to cultural change. It empowers individuals not just to begin, but to endure. It signals to teams that setbacks are not dead ends—they're checkpoints. And it creates the conditions for sustained growth, where long-term thinking and gritty follow-through replace short-term panic and abandonment.

This kind of persistence is deeply human. It's the muscle we all carry, even when we forget it's there. It's what makes the next step possible, even when the summit is out of sight.

Examples of Growth Mindset Rituals at Work

Here are some real-life rituals that reflect key areas of the Growth Mindset. These are how organizations begin to scale persistence, adaptability, and learning. They don't motivate people to behave differently. They remove the need to *decide* to behave differently:

Growth Area	**Ritual in Practice**
Beliefs	"Future-You": step into the future version of yourself as a leader, not just in title. Visualize how others experience your leadership and work backwards.
Risk-Taking	"Small Bets" challenges to reward bold, early experiments.
Challenges	"Learning Questions: "What was our hardest moment and what did we learn?"
Effort	"Weekly Ship": ship unfinished work weekly to your key stakeholders so you can improve the work based on their insights.
Success of Others	"Gratitude Journal": Friday recognitions for invisible contributions, not just outcomes.
Feedback	"Demo Meeting" with leadership to normalize transparency.
Failure	Quarterly "Failure Resume" roundtable for shared learning.
Persistence	"Mid-week Action Meetings": stand-ups to surface and unblock challenges.

Scan the QR codes below to access short RESET Leader videos that help you recognize growth barriers, shift mindsets, and experiment with new habits.

Growth Area: Persistence

Discover how rhythm, focus, and commitment help you sustain progress—especially when the work gets hard or repetitive.

https://qr.resetleader.com/gUjJboUU

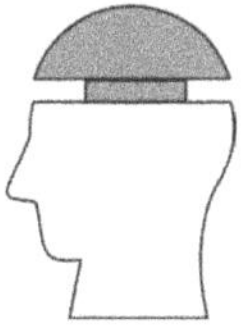

In Closing ...

Writing this book has been more than an intellectual endeavor; it has been a personal reckoning. Through years of working with leaders across industries and continents, we've seen how growth is rarely blocked by a lack of strategy or talent—it's blocked by the mindsets we leave unchallenged, and this book is a response to that reality, and an invitation to reflect and shift mindsets and behaviors that no longer work for you. It doesn't matter if you are a leader at a large Fortune 500 company or a small family-owned business, a start-up or a nonprofit—the RESET framework is about empowering the teams, managers, and individuals in your organization to be their best, most productive selves.

R - Recognize Growth Barriers: Spot the patterns and behaviors that no longer serve you, the habits that slow momentum and hold you back from executing your strategy.

E – Evaluate Mindset Shifts: Look beneath the surface. Identify the forces that shape those behaviors and reframe them to open new pathways for growth.

S – Set Up Habit-Shifting Experiments: Turn intention into action. Design small, bold tests and practices to challenge old routines and build new ways of working.

E – Examine New Behavior Impact: Pause to learn. Measure what's changing, notice what's working, and refine what moves you closer to meaningful progress.

T – Transform Successful Habits into New Working Rituals: Make changes stick. Embed the habits that drive success into your rhythm, culture, and daily leadership practices.

The five steps of the RESET process are meant to guide this shift. They help leaders and teams to recognize what holds you back, question the beliefs behind your actions, experiment with new behaviors, and transform what works into lasting rituals. These steps are not theory; they are a practice, a way to turn reflection into action, and action into meaningful execution and sustainable results.

RESET is not just a methodology. It's an operating system that touches all levels of your organization. It is a mindset that encourages growth. A practical rhythm that delivers reflection, and results. When these five steps become part of how you show up at work and in your daily life, you don't simply respond to change—you accelerate your growth through it. The proof does not live in these pages, but in your pauses, your choices, and the shifts you create—and the results you achieve.

But we have to be honest with ourselves: Like anything else, RESET won't immediately erase the barriers to growth or the natural pulls and reflexes that make us human. The fear of failure. The sting of criticism. The allure of what's familiar. It is important to acknowledge that these behaviors and emotions will still come; this is inevitable. What RESET offers is a different way to meet them—to pause, to breathe, to notice, and to choose again. You're not here to become perfect. You're here to become comfortable with stretching yourself in uncomfortable territory, to embrace change and roll with it. The alternative is to stay rooted in the past even as the future leaves you behind.

We live in the tension between dualities, between the self that reacts and the self that reflects. Between the mountaintop that inspires us and the valley that transforms us. Leadership isn't about escaping that tension; it's about learning to hold it with grace and setting an example for others, to model the change we want to see.

What I've come to understand is that RESET doesn't stop at work. While I wrote this book for leaders, transformation rarely respects these boundaries. During one of the hardest seasons of my life—walking through the pain of separation and rebuilding from the ground up—I found myself applying these same principles. Reflecting on what no longer works. Understanding what contributed to this change.

Experimenting with what comes next and holding on to what works—and then beginning again, in a continuous process of RESET. For me, it opened the door to something deeper: a spiritual grounding that reminded me that renewal doesn't come from control, but from surrender.

So as you take RESET into your own work, I encourage you to look beyond that and notice where else in your life it can make a difference: in your relationships, your health, your faith, your identity. Wherever life is asking you to release, to reflect, and to start again—that's where the RESET begins.

If you take only a single truth from these pages, let it be this one: Growth is not a destination or an endstate. It's a posture. A readiness to see, to stretch, to shift, and to show up differently.

So revisit the rituals and the questions they pose to you. Share and reflect on your insights. Start the conversations that you've been avoiding. Invite your team, your friends, your family into the RESET journey with you. Let your next courageous act be proof of your transformation, and become the growth that you want to see.

Because when RESET becomes more than a tool, when it becomes your way of living and leading, what you gain is more than results.

You gain clarity.

You gain freedom.

You gain peace.

You become your future self.

Always remember that while the mountaintop is what inspires us, the valley below is what transforms us.

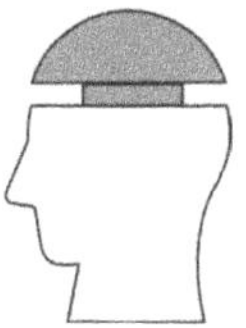

Acknowledgements

Writing this book has been both a privilege and a responsibility, like leadership itself. It has been a journey filled with momentum, doubt, learning, and growth. While it is my name that appears on the cover, this book is the result of many people who believed, challenged, contributed, and walked alongside me over the years, and who helped me reach the understandings that today influence almost everything that I do.

First, I want to thank the leaders who trusted us early and pushed us to deliver impact that would last. In particular, I'm deeply grateful to Tuncay Özgüner, whose trust and willingness to test, experiment, and learn gave us permission to explore paths that simply wouldn't have existed otherwise. Many organizations benefit from that openness today, and you've been a critical mentor in sharpening what truly matters for business—especially in those moments when I was deep in the details and needed to be lifted back up to first principles. Your often-repeated question, "What is the end-game?" has a remarkable way of cutting through complexity and restoring clarity. And among the many quotes that might justify a book of their own, one made it all the way into print on one of our graduation notebooks: "Start as a Turk, keep going as a Dutchman, and finish it off as a German." That blend of drive, pragmatism, and discipline captures your influence perfectly—and continues to guide how we work today.

To the thousands of *Growthstars* (professionals who graduated from our Growth Mindset Accelerators), the leaders and professionals who have walked this journey with us: *Thank you*. You were never "participants" or "clients"; you were collaborators. Through your openness, resistance, feedback, and willingness to experiment, you shaped what RESET has become. Much of what's in this book exists because of what we learned together—through trial, error, reflection, and progress.

I also want to express my deepest appreciation to my partner Otto Freijser, whose role as COO has been instrumental in turning ideas into reality. Since our foundation, Otto elevated not only our delivery, but the way we facilitate, coach, and scale impact across engagements. Your steadiness, insight, and commitment to excellence helped translate vision into execution, again and again. Through your leadership, what began as a Growth Mindset program evolved into the operating system that *RESET Leader* is today—bringing coherence, scale, and durability to our work, and ensuring impact that holds over time.

To Timo Hamoen, our CTO: Thank you for building what others could only imagine. The *RESET Leader* application exists because of your ability to translate complex ideas into clear, reliable software architecture, turning ambition into something usable, scalable, and human. You translated vision into software with a deep sense of responsibility for the people this system is meant to serve. Through your work, our deliverables became stronger and more consistent, and the coaches and mentors who use the system are better equipped to do their best work. Your work carries the weight of our purpose, helping *RESET Leader* reach far beyond what any of us could do alone.

I'm also deeply grateful to Edwin van Vianen and Josh Simmons, our first accredited professional coaches. Beyond challenging our thinking and pushing for practical value, you helped us deliver *RESET Leader* where it truly matters—in real leadership contexts. Your work shaped what accreditation stands for in practice, ensuring that *RESET Leader* serves not just organizations, but the professionals who bring it to life every day.

Finally, to everyone I may be forgetting to mention—partners, collaborators, team members, clients, and supporters—this book came to life over the past three years through countless conversations, sessions, pilots, and moments of shared learning. If you see yourself reflected in these pages, know that your contribution mattered.

Leadership, growth, and transformation are never solo efforts.

This book is proof of that.

Thank you,
—Mesut

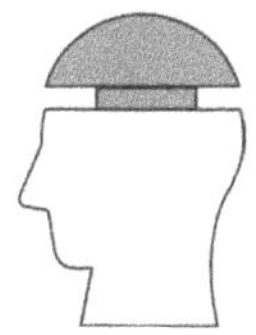

About the Author

Mesut Celebi is the founder of **Growthstars**, a leadership firm that activates strategy into execution at speed through its RESET OS.

Mesut began his career in the Netherlands in the packaging industry before transitioning to entrepreneurship and founding his first company in 1999. Over the next two decades, he co-founded and scaled numerous companies in industrial technology, manufacturing, and software across Europe, Africa, and the Middle East. His work in multiple sectors and industries gave him a broad perspective on how global companies grow, scale, and operate in different markets and cultures.

In 2009, after moving to New York, he co-founded Startupbootcamp USA, a global start-up accelerator, where he applied the entrepreneurial lessons at scale to support new innovations and technologies. Through this work,

Mesut observed a consistent pattern: Strategies often fail not because they lack clarity, but because the underlying behaviors and mindsets that drive day-to-day decisions remain unexamined. He saw the same thing as a senior partner with Innoleaps, an innovation agency for enterprises, where the similar patterns appeared time and time again.

This realization led him to develop the **RESET** framework: a practical, five-step method that helps leaders recognize their growth barriers, evaluate mindset shifts, set up habit-shifting experiments, examine their impact, and transform successful habits into new working rituals.

RESET Leader distills Mesut's experience from years of building organizations, working with leadership teams, and accelerating strategy execution into an accessible and actionable method that can be used by anyone. Today, he focuses on expanding the RESET methodology through programs, products, and partnerships that equip leaders to drive lasting transformation in their teams and organizations.

To learn more about Mesut and his work, connect with him by scanning the QR code below:

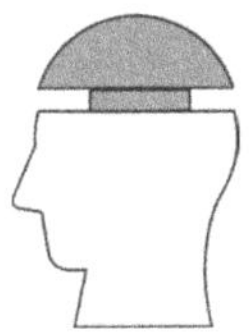

Hire Mesut to Speak

Create lasting impact at your next leadership event with Mesut Celebi as your keynote speaker.

With more than two decades as a founder and investor, with experience across startups, scale-ups, and multinational organizations, Mesut brings a grounded, real-world perspective on how leaders and businesses grow at speed.

His keynotes focus on how beliefs, habits, and everyday decisions shape performance—especially when pressure is high and the path forward is unclear.

His sessions consistently leave leaders with a renewed sense of ownership, adaptability, and confidence to lead through uncertainty, and serve as the springboard for navigating change.

To learn more about booking Mesut for a keynote, leadership offsite, or executive event, visit www.MesutCelebi.com or www.ResetLeader.com.

Ask Mesut to speak about:

- Why smart strategies fail—and what leaders must unlearn to make change stick
- How leaders build momentum when certainty disappears and pressure rises
- Turning resistance into a signal for growth instead of a barrier to progress
- What it really takes to shift behavior, not just alignment, in leadership teams
- Leading organizations that learn faster than the pace of change
- Breaking fixed mindsets that quietly slow execution
- RESET Leadership: how great leaders pause, reflect, and reset before moving forward
- Building resilience and responsiveness as a daily leadership practice—not a crisis response

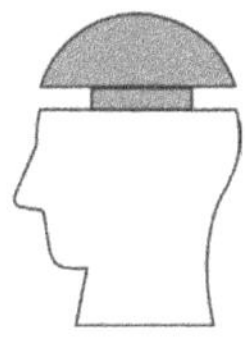

About Growthstars

Growthstars exists to close one of the most persistent gaps in organizations today: the gap between strategy and execution.

That gap is rarely caused by a lack of plans, skills, or training. It exists because the underlying operating system leaders and teams rely on—their mindsets, decision patterns, and behavioral defaults—was built for a more stable world. In today's continuously changing work reality, those defaults quietly slow execution, reduce adaptability, and weaken ownership.

Growthstars brings an operating system for leadership and teams—*RESET Leader*—that makes mindset visible, measurable, and actionable at scale. Rather than delivering training or running programs, we provide a structured system that helps organizations understand how leaders and teams think, respond, and perform under pressure.

At the core of this system is a mindset assessment that reveals the beliefs and behaviors shaping execution. It shows where teams demonstrate resilience, learning capacity, and responsiveness—and where they default to habits that limit adaptability in moments of uncertainty and change.

This measurement turns abstract concepts like "Growth Mindset" into concrete leadership data. It creates a shared language for leadership teams, enabling sharper alignment, faster decisions, and more effective collaboration across functions and boundaries.

Based on these insights, we work with senior leaders to reset the operating system that drives day-to-day behavior. The focus is not on motivation or compliance, but on enabling leaders and teams to think and act differently—consistently, under pressure, and over time.

The *RESET Leader* operating system is designed to embed into everyday leadership work. It supports organizations as they navigate constant change, competing priorities, and rising complexity—without adding another layer of initiatives or frameworks.

Growthstars operates globally, partnering with organizations that are serious about turning strategy into action and building resilient, responsive organizations that can sustain performance in continuous change.

For more information, tools, and resources visit us at: www.growthstars.co or scan the QR code below:

www.ingramcontent.com/pod-product-compliance
Lightning Source LLC
Chambersburg PA
CBHW041937150726
48192CB00024B/119

* 9 7 9 8 8 8 7 9 7 2 2 9 9 *